'For Civilisation'

The First World War in the Middle East 1914-1923

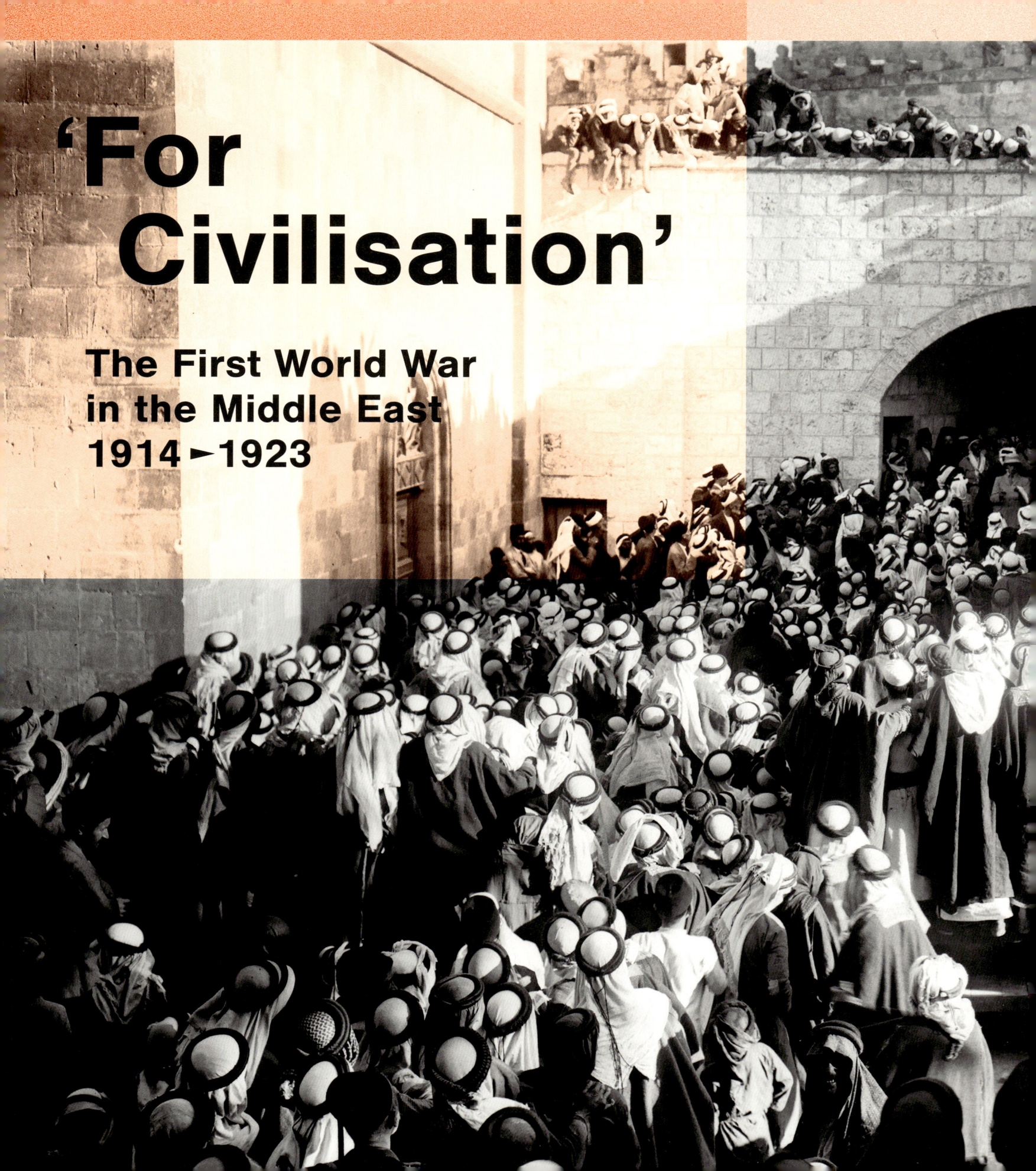

'For Civilisation'

The First World War in the Middle East 1914▶1923

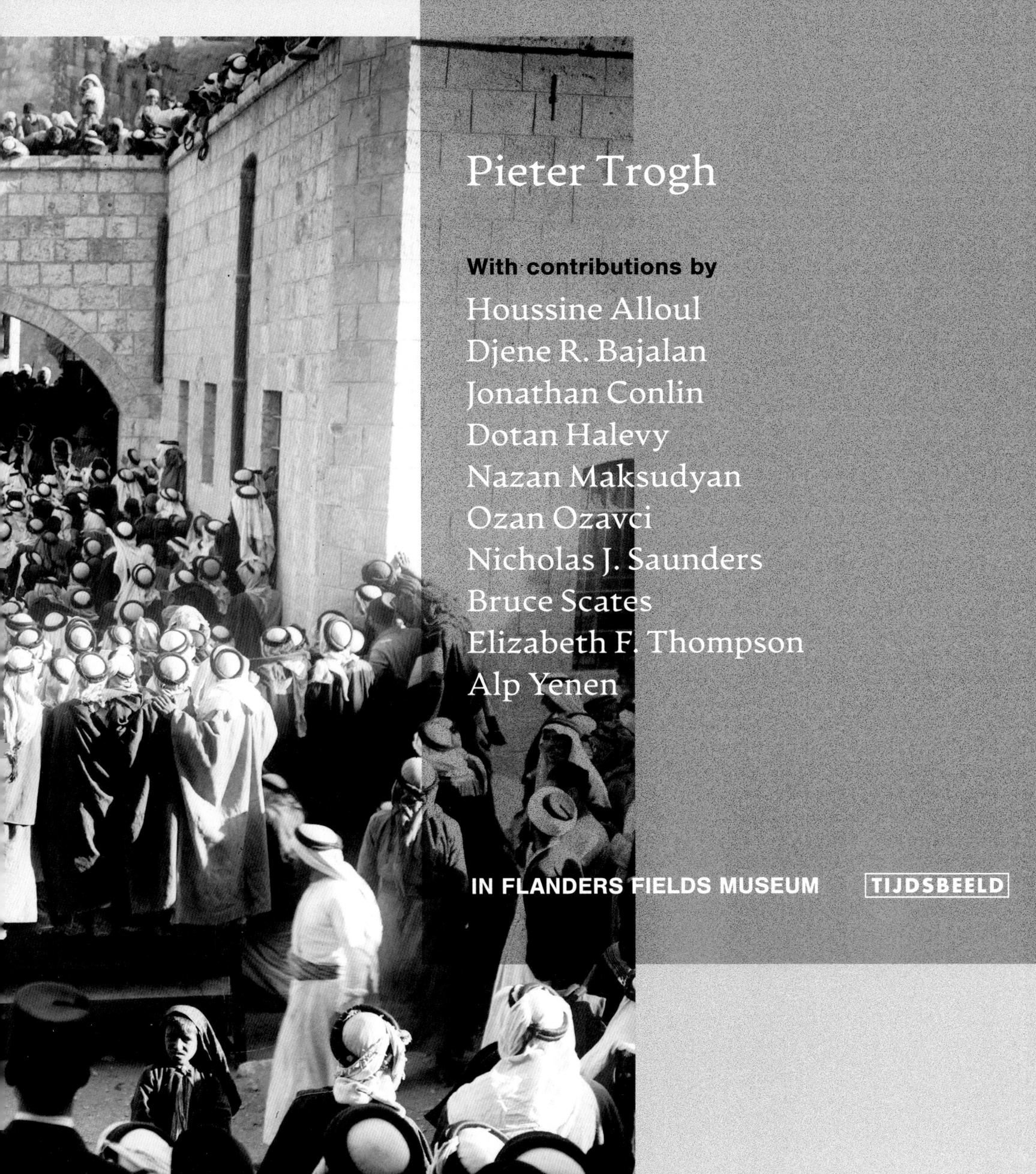

Pieter Trogh

With contributions by

Houssine Alloul
Djene R. Bajalan
Jonathan Conlin
Dotan Halevy
Nazan Maksudyan
Ozan Ozavci
Nicholas J. Saunders
Bruce Scates
Elizabeth F. Thompson
Alp Yenen

IN FLANDERS FIELDS MUSEUM   TIJDSBEELD

introduction
Pieter Trogh
'For Civilisation':
the First World War
in the Middle East,
1914–1923 6

story
Theodor Wiegand 12

images
A Fascination with the East .. 14

essay
Houssine Alloul
Belgium and the Ottoman
Empire in the Long
Nineteenth Century 24

essay
Pieter Trogh
From Declarations of
War to Armistice:
The First World War in
the Middle East, 1914–1918 ... 30

story
Falih Rıfkı 36

essay
Pieter Trogh
Wavell's Eye: Connections
between Flanders Fields
and the Middle East
in the First World War 38

story
Frank Hurley 44

images
**Waging War
in the Middle East** 48

story
Shenorhig Tenguerian 76

essay
Nazan Maksudyan
Gendered Violence
against Children during
the Armenian Genocide 78

story
Ihsan Turjman 84

story
Alp Yenen
Between Imperialism and
Revolution: Geopolitics
of the Great War
in the Middle East 86

story
Faisal 92

essay
Nicholas J. Saunders
The Pillars of Belief:
T. E. Lawrence and the
archaeology of the Arab
Revolt, 1916–2014 94

images
People 100

essay
Ozan Ozavci
Sèvres, Lausanne, and
the Invention of the
Middle East 122

story
Halide Edib 128

essay
Elizabeth F. Thompson
The Arab Liberal Revolutions
of 1919 and the Violent
Consequences of
European Suppression 130

images
Places 136

essay
Bruce Scates
Victor and Vanquished:
Contested War Memory
in the Middle East 158

story
George Knox 164

essay
Dotan Halevy
The First World War and the
Zionist-Palestinian Conflict,
1914–1948 166

story
Wasif Jawhariyyeh 172

essay
Djene R. Bajalan
The Kurds and
the First World War 174

story
Gertrude Bell 180

essay
Jonathan Conlin
Oil: A Crude History
of the Great War 182

Further Reading 188

About the authors 190

Contents

Pieter TROGH

'For Civilisation': the First World War in the Middle East, 1914–1923

The 'Middle East' features regularly in the news. All too frequently in the form of war reports or accounts of tensions between different groups of people. Trying to trace the origins of those conflicts often leads us to the First World War.

In the West the guns fell silent on 11 November 1918, but for various reasons fighting continued in the Middle East until 1923. When war broke out in 1914, the region was largely dominated by the Ottoman Empire, then under the regime of the Young Turks. They had allied with Germany and so found themselves on the losing side in 1918. The Ottoman Empire disintegrated, and the borders were redrawn to suit the interests of Great Britain and France. That process caused considerable ill feeling among the people and communities living in the Middle East. Conflicts were created then that have continued to smoulder and can still flare up into new violence even today. We need only think of the Israeli-Palestinian conflict, for instance, or the fate of the Kurds, or the fraught relationship between Turks and Armenians, over which the legacy of the Armenian Genocide hangs like a black cloud. But in general terms, too, the impact of the First World War on the Middle East was enormous: the people who lived there lost many opportunities. If we want a better understanding of present relationships and the balance of power in the Middle East, we must go back to the First World War and its aftermath.

This book re-examines the impact on and legacy of that war in the Middle East. It is part of a project initiated by In Flanders Fields Museum in Ypres in 2022 to explore that subject and is conceived as a popular history book, published on the occasion of the exhibition entitled *'For Civilisation'. the First World War in the Middle East, 1914–1923*. In short and accessible essays, ten experts expand on a number of themes that were dealt with in the exhibition. A select bibliography directs interested readers to the more specialised literature.

Houssine Alloul sheds light on the multifaceted relationships between Belgium and the Ottoman Empire during the long nineteenth century. The geopolitical game played out in the region during the First World War is outlined by Alp Yenen, while Ozan Ozavci examines the shaping of the modern Middle East in the war's aftermath. Nicholas J. Saunders investigates the role of T. E. Lawrence (aka Lawrence of Arabia) from an archaeological-cum-anthropological perspective, and Bruce Scates describes the contentious creation of the commemorative landscape of the First World War in the Middle East. Nazan Maksudyan looks at the Armenian Genocide, but from a child's perspective. Dotan Halevy goes back to the origins of the Israeli-Palestinian question by interpreting the Zionist project in Palestine between 1914 and 1948. Djene R. Bajalan examines the fate of the Kurds during the First World War

Angled aerial view of the pyramids at Giza in Egypt, taken from a military observation aircraft, 1915

'The Mediterranean without Borders' is an artistic creation by Sabine Réthoré. There are many ways of looking at the world, including this region. Or, as the artist states: 'I did not draw the borders that divide us, but the thousands of roads that connect us.'

and its aftermath. Jonathan Conlin discusses the importance and legacy of the discovery of oil in the region. Elizabeth F. Thompson's essay is devoted to the wave of liberal revolutions that took place in Arab countries in 1919 and the violent consequences that followed their suppression by Western powers. By way of introduction, the present author gives a brief survey of crucial events and evolutions between 1914 and 1918, and in a further essay he offers a view of the connections between Flanders Fields and the Middle East as seen through the prism of the First World War. Punctuating the chapters is a series of extraordinary personal narratives that turn this multifaceted history into a people's story.

The Middle East

Today 'the Middle East' is a commonly used construct, but what does it mean and where does it come from? Geographically speaking, 'Middle East' generally denotes the Islamic world that lies largely between the Mediterranean Sea and the Persian Gulf. The term can also be interpreted politically and historically. The name 'Middle East' originated around 1900, at the height of the colonial expansion of what were then the global British and French empires, when Western Europe was regarded the centre of the world. Thus, the terms 'Near East', 'Middle East', and 'Far East' refer to their location in relation to the dominant West. Indeed, so commanding was the West's position that even today the inhabitants of the area themselves still use an Arabic translation of the imported term 'Middle East' (ash-Sharq al-Awsaṭ).

The Middle East is the cradle of many ancient cultures and civilisations, those of the West included. Large parts of the area fell within the Greek sphere of influence and the Roman Empire, and there, too, the biblical stories of the Holy Land have their origin. In the West, the period between roughly 1860 and 1914 saw a sharp increase in interest in that history, and the area became more easily accessible. Many Western historians, archaeologists, artists, adventurers, linguists, and ethnologists set out on expeditions to the Middle East, known then primarily as 'the Orient', a concept that was associated with exoticism. The fascination exerted by that chimeric Orient dominated Western thinking and its image of 'the Middle East'. The Orient was, as it were, a construct onto which the desires (and fears) of the West were projected. That was certainly the case in the arts and literature. Besides, adherents of Western view naturally considered it superior to the Eastern. In geopolitical reality, the region tended to be regarded as a land to be exploited, ripe for European expansion. And since it was seen from that perspective, knowledge of the Orient was inextricably linked to the imperialist societies who produced it, as Edward Said argues in his classic work *Orientalism*.

As a concept, 'Middle East' belittles that region's unifying importance—geographic, cultural, and economic—in world history. The historian Rashid Khalidi has frequently criticised the one-sided analytical framework created by the West: not only is it archaic and misleading, but it also condemns the region to being seen solely through the eyes and interests of others, mainly Westerners. In the Middle East itself, however, there are other descriptions of the region that start from alternative worldviews and world histories than those of the West. There are, for example, the Arabic terms 'Arabic world' (*al-alam al-Arabi*) and 'Islamic world' (*al-alam al-Islami*), or the more loaded descriptions 'Arab community' (*al-umma al-Arabiyya*) and 'Islamic

Pieter Trogh 'For Civilisation'

8

Meeting between Bedouins and German soldiers from a medical unit, Damascus, Syria, c. 1914

community' (*al-umma al-Islamiyya*). Such designations provide powerful alternative frameworks for describing and understanding the area. Based on an idea of world history seen from a Muslim perspective, Tamim Ansary has coined the term 'Middle World'.

Besides the actual term itself, Rashid Khalidi sees other problems with the 'Middle East' label, one of them being the lack of a precise definition of the areas, countries, cultures, religions, and language groups it covers. On that issue there is no consensus. Some definitions include North Africa, others do not. Likewise, Turkey, Iran, Afghanistan, and so on. The only areas included in virtually every definition of the 'Middle East' are the present-day countries that belonged to the 'Fertile Crescent' and the Arabian Peninsula: Iraq, Syria, Lebanon, Jordan, Israel, Palestine, and Saudi Arabia. This book is mainly about that region—and Turkey, Egypt, and Armenia too. In 1914, those areas were largely under Ottoman rule. They were front lines and scenes of genocidal violence during the First World War.

Another (Western) misconception about the Middle East relates to the (religious) identity of the people who live there. For many Westerners, the Middle East is synonymous with 'Islam'. That one-sided view does grave injustice to the many millions of non-Muslims in the region: Copts in Egypt; Israeli Jews; Christians of various eastern and western denominations in Palestine, Lebanon, Syria, and Iraq; followers of other faiths, such as the Yezidis, or adherents of Baha'i teachings. (It also ignores the fact that the vast majority of Muslims live outside the Middle East.) Khalidi's dissection of the 'Middle East' as an analytical framework for the region exposes the misconceptions and prejudices shared by many in the Western world today. Such views were also ubiquitous during the first months of the war in 1914. Like the Germans, the British contemplated exploiting 'the Muslims' of the Ottoman Empire to further their own military objectives. David Fromkin explains the reasoning of British Commander-in-Chief Lord Herbert Kitchener as follows:

> 'Kitchener, like most Britons who lived in the East, believed that in the Moslem world religion counts for everything ... They mistakenly seemed to believe that Mohammedism was a centralized, authoritarian structure. They regarded Islam as a single entity: as an "it", as an organisation. They believed that "it" obeyed its leaders ... Kitchener and his colleagues believed that Islam could be bought, manipulated, or captured by buying, manipulating, or capturing its religious leadership.'

There is often an echo of contempt to be heard in the misconceptions and prejudices about the Middle East. One of the low points of Western disdain for the region dates from 1993, when the American political scientist Samuel P. Huntington published his influential article 'The Clash of Civilizations'. Huntington saw cultural and religious identity as the greatest source of global conflict in the post-Cold War period. The history of mankind, he maintained, was one of successive civilisations, with Western civilisation remaining as the superior victor. In Huntington's narrative the Islamic civilisation and world are described in an extraordinarily derogatory way. 'Islam'—as a religion and a culture—is represented as utterly alienated, monolithic, and unchanging, with a history of continuous conflict between the Islamic world and all its neighbours. Although Huntington's theory has been repeatedly and convincingly debunked as ahistorical and reductionist, his view continues to resonate in the West. The fact that many causes of the tensions and conflicts in the Middle East bear a Western stamp—a stamp (among other things) that was struck in the period between 1914 and 1923—is ignored or minimised by Islamophobes or adherents of the 'clashing civilisations' model.

The Inter-Allied Medal, also known as the 'Victory Medal', was awarded to around 11 million veterans from the Allied countries after the First World War. In Belgium, it was awarded to more than 300,000 servicemen. Archives of the Royal Palace, Brussels

'For Civilisation'

After 1918, millions of veterans from the various Allied armies were awarded the so-called Inter-Allied Victory Medal. On the obverse is the full-length figure of Nike, the ancient Greek goddess of victory. On the reverse can be read—in the language (or languages) of the fifteen nations in which the medal was awarded—this inscription: THE / GREAT WAR / FOR CIVILISATION / 1914–1919. Judging the course of the First World War and its pernicious settlements by this slogan begs the question: For which civilisation? Whose civilisation? When news of the numerous atrocities committed by the German army against the civilian population of Belgium and northern France in the first months of the war became known, Allied war propaganda eagerly seized on it to spin the idea of a just war 'for civilisation' (and 'against barbarism') on the home front. Moreover, for many Commonwealth servicemen who had fought in the Middle East during the war, that conceptual civilisation gave worthwhile meaning to their wartime experience: they imagined that they had 'brought civilisation' to a world which they believed to be inferior. In reality, the slogan cast a camouflaging veil over a war that was largely based on colonialist and imperialist motives. At the same time, there were many on the Allied side who were quite certain that their European culture stemmed from ancient Rome and Christianity, and thus derived from the cradles of civilisation, particularly Greece and the Middle East. The Allies claimed the right to defend 'their' Western civilisation. Exporting the European world war to said cradle, however, was not so much a sign of admiration but primarily of a deeply entrenched belief in European supremacy and its 'civilising mission'. That conclusion is reminiscent of what the French-Lebanese writer Amin Maalouf calls the (seemingly timeless) 'opposing ambitions of the West'—between 'civilising and dominating'.

'The West is constantly caught between two completely opposite ambitions, wanting to 'civilise' the rest of the world and at the same time to dominate it. Those are two things that are impossible to combine. If you want to give the other more dignity, education, and freedom, you run the risk that the other will no longer allow himself to be subordinated. The division between westerners who live in prosperity and indigenous people who must survive without even the bare minimum is incompatible with Western values.' (MO *Magazine*, 30 September 2009)

The cynicism of the Inter-Allied Victory Medal has inspired the titles of several projects. Just as British journalist Robert Fisk did when titling his magnum opus (*The Great War For Civilisation: The Conquest of the Middle East*, 2005), this book (and the exhibition in IFFM) also takes the text on the reverse of the medal as the basis for questioning 'the Great War For Civilisation'.

The Ottoman Empire

In 1914, the Middle East lay largely under the rule of the centuries-old Ottoman Empire. By then it was only a fraction of the size it had been at its height in the seventeenth century. The expansionism of great powers such as France, Britain, and Russia had led to the Ottoman loss of parts of Central Europe and North Africa. The Ottoman government's increasingly precarious financial situation also made its responses less and less decisive. The emergence of new, European-style nationalisms and increasing interference by foreign imperial powers like Austria and Russia (and later Italy) prompted uprisings. Several population groups—such as the Greeks, Serbs, Montenegrins, Romanians, and Bulgarians—declared their independence. In the meantime, Western powers gained an ever-growing influence in the Empire's domestic affairs, and foreign investors acquired dominant positions in its economy.

Pieter Trogh   'For Civilisation'

Inspection of Ottoman troops, 1914

Internally, the second half of the nineteenth century had seen the Empire undergo a difficult process of modernisation and centralisation. Progressives tried to push through reforms but were thwarted by conservative groups. In 1876, a democratic parliament was established and a constitution drawn up, only to be suspended not long afterwards by the new sultan, Abdulhamid II. Under his policy, certain groups became increasingly frustrated by the compromise between patrimonial traditionalism and modernisation, while foreign interference continued to grow. One of the best-organised groups was the secular and patriotic Committee of Union and Progress, better known in Europe as the 'Young Turks'. In 1908, they staged a first coup in which they restored the constitution, argued for a parliamentary democracy, and proposed the ending of all manner of privileges vis-à-vis foreign interference. Between 1909 and 1912, conservative agencies tried to re-establish their predominant position, but in 1913 the Young Turks staged a violent coup d'état that finally gave them power in Constantinople. They installed a triumvirate with Enver Pasha, Djemal Pasha, and Talaat Pasha, who sought to counter the difficulties of the empire with a Turkish nationalist ideology. In 1914 the Young Turks kept a close eye on rising tensions in Europe. If war broke out, it could create opportunities to further develop the Ottoman Empire into a strong and modern state. To achieve this end, the Young Turks concluded that a strategic alliance with one of the great powers would be necessary, but they were divided over which it should be. Great Britain, France, and Germany were all considered. In the end, the choice fell on Germany as the best ally. The Germans offered money and military support and showed no colonial interest in their empire. The Ottomans were also convinced that Germany would win the war.

Theodor WIEGAND

1864–1936

In 1914, after much hesitation, the Ottoman Empire finally formed an alliance with the German Empire. It was not entirely surprising. For decades the two empires had maintained good diplomatic, military, and economic relations. The high point of Ottoman-German cooperation was undoubtedly the appointing of German engineers and firms to build a railway link between Berlin and Baghdad. Work started in 1903 but was interrupted by the outbreak of war. At that point the railway line was still some 900 kilometres short of Baghdad. Those good relations enabled the Germans to extract privileges in certain fields while the petitions of other Westerners were denied. One of those fields was archaeology. In 1899, thanks to a secret imperial Ottoman decree, German researchers and archaeologists were given generous exploitation rights in excavations. The results of German archaeological diligence between 1900 and 1914 can still be seen today in the museums on the Museum Island in Berlin.

One of the key figures in that process was the German archaeologist Theodor Wiegand, who, between 1899 and 1911, represented a number of Berlin museums as foreign director in Constantinople. Thanks to Wiegand, German museums acquired countless reliefs, friezes, and smaller archaeological objects from excavations in Pergamon, Priene, Miletus and Didyma, as well as via the art trade and from private collections. When war broke out, Wiegand hoped that these activities could still go on as before. He persuaded the German and Ottoman authorities that the protection of 'endangered archaeological monuments' was important. In 1916, a special *Denkmalschutzkommando* or 'historic monument protection unit' was established that would document, collect, and restore historical heritage behind Ottoman lines. Djemal Pasha, commander of the Ottoman troops in Syria and Palestine, saw in this project an opportunity to modernise the preservation of monuments in the empire and to strengthen 'Ottoman identity'. Ottoman archaeologists such as Halil Edhem Eldem were rather more sceptical about the German idea of preservation, seeing it more as looting.

Between 1916 and 1918, Wiegand's unit carried out extensive inventory work. Numerous ancient monuments in present-day Syria, Lebanon, Israel, and Jordan were measured and photographed in detail. In various respects the German archaeologists were able to work in conditions that were very much better than 'in peacetime'. When military observation aircraft were deployed, for instance, it was the first time that aerial photography was used on such a scale for archaeological research. Both during and after the war, Wiegand published several books about his research, as well as two photographic albums. Ironically, a hundred years later his work would not be out of place among the initiatives aimed at the digital (or 3D) reconstruction of heritage sites in Syria that were destroyed by the IS terrorist organisation, of which Palmyra is undoubtedly the best known.

Portrait of Theodor Wiegand, c. 1930

13 Ruins of Palmyra (Syria), c. 1898 Theodor Wiegand

In the decades before the war, Paul Vandenpeereboom (sitting, with cap), who came from Kortrijk (Courtrai), undertook several 'pilgrimages' to the Holy Land. He brought together his experiences in a richly illustrated travelogue. In this photograph he is on a ship from Port Said (Egypt) to Jaffa (Palestine).

15

Bustle at the station
in Homs (Syria), c. 1898

Snapshots from Paul Vandenpeerenboom's travelogue recounting his 'pilgrimages' to the Holy Land, with pictures taken in Athens, Cairo, Jerusalem, Hebron, and Aswan, *c.* 1910

Photograph of an Egyptian woman in Cairo, c. 1910, from the collection of Paul Vandenpeerenboom

An Arab cafe in Cairo, c. 1910, from the collection of Paul Vandenpeerenboom

A Market in Aswan, Egypt, *c.* 1910, from the collection of Paul Vandenpeerenboom

Inside a spinning mill in Beirut, Lebanon, *c.* 1910, from the collection of Paul Vandenpeerenboom

The site of Karnak, Egypt, c. 1910

The Nymphaeum (ancient monument dedicated to the nymphs) at Amman, Jordan, c. 1910

20

21

The site of Giza, Egypt, c. 1910.

Thomas Edward Lawrence (1888–1935) was involved in several archaeological digs in the Middle East before the war. In 1915, owing to his knowledge of the region and its languages and culture, Lawrence was assigned to British intelligence in Cairo.

A lone traveller with his camel in the Sinai Desert, 1910

Edouard Empain was a prominent Belgian entrepeneur. One of his most prestigious projects was the luxurious Heliopolis district, close to the Egyptian capital of Cairo, developed in the decade before the war. The Hindu Palace was Empain's own residence in Heliopolis.

Houssine Alloul

Houssine ALLOUL

Belgium and the Ottoman Empire in the Long Nineteenth Century

When German forces invaded Belgium on 4 August 1914, the Ottoman government had already concluded an alliance with the German Empire. Istanbul kept out of the war until October, when a military campaign was launched against Russia. In response, on 5 November, Russia, France, and Great Britain declared war on the Ottomans. Belgium and the Ottoman Empire suddenly found themselves on opposite sides and broke off diplomatic relations, but without a declaration of war in either direction. It might seem surprising that there should have been any diplomatic relations at all between two such different states, but before the breach of 1914 there was a long prior history of intense economic, cultural, and political exchange. Here I will examine this rich history and show how the Great War and its immediate aftermath radically altered relations between Belgians and Ottomans.

Tightening the Bonds

The official history of Ottoman-Belgian relations begins in 1838, the year in which the two states signed a commercial treaty in Istanbul. Belgian policymakers hoped to find new, lucrative markets for their country's rapidly developing industry and to get a foot in the door of the Ottoman capital, which at that moment was one of Europe's diplomatic focal points. For Sultan Mahmud II and his government, Belgium was an attractive new trading partner and a potential counterweight to their growing economic dependence on an imperialist Great Britain and, to a lesser extent, France.

The formalisation of contacts between Brussels and Istanbul did not mean that there had not been earlier trading relations. A flourishing traffic in goods between the Southern Netherlands and the great ports of the eastern Mediterranean was already going on in the late Middle Ages. In the industrial era, even before Belgian independence in 1830, Istanbul looked with great interest at the pioneering role of Southern Netherlandish companies in the mechanical mass production of textiles, steel, weapons, and machines. In the 1820s, when the Ottomans were fighting against rebels in the Peloponnese, several contracts were agreed with gunmakers in Liège. René Spitaels, a Belgian traveller who lived in the Ottoman capital from August 1837 to February 1838, noted in his travel journal: 'People in Belgium would be very surprised to learn that our country supplies the grappling hooks for the Grand Turk's entire fleet. I was able to ascertain with some satisfaction that the Liège hallmark is highly regarded here.' Commercial connections such as these paved the way for the 1838 treaty and explain why Belgium sent a representative to the Ottoman court as early as 1839. Istanbul reciprocated ten years later, when the Ottoman Empire opened a legation in Brussels. This was only their sixth permanent embassy abroad, after those in Paris, London, Vienna, Berlin, and Athens. In the following years, both countries established several consulates on each other's territory.

In the third quarter of the nineteenth century, bonds were tightened further. Arms manufacturers in Liège were among the Ottoman army's major suppliers. This was also

Studio portrait of Mehmed Kâmil Bey from the collection of Leopold II and a souvenir of his trip to Istanbul in 1860. Archives of the Royal Palace, Brussels

Bilingual advertisement (1911–14) for the Société Franco-Belge de Matériel de Chemins de Fer, in which Belgians had a majority share. The advertisement shows a model railway wagon delivered to a mining company in Ereğli (Zonguldak) in the Ottoman Empire.

the period when a select number of Belgian and Ottoman merchant houses established branches in Istanbul and Antwerp, respectively. They played an important role in mediating commercial and financial exchanges between the two countries. The Helbigs from Liège, for example, enjoyed considerable renown in the Ottoman capital. They had an extensive property portfolio and were important money lenders for the Ottoman authorities. Traces of this Belgian presence can still be seen in Istanbul, most notably in the luxury apartment complex that Charles Helbig had built in Galata (Karaköy), now known as Doğan Apartmanı. From the 1850s onwards, Istanbul provided dozens of scholarships for students to attend the prestigious École Royale Militaire in Brussels. In later decades, many other young Ottomans found their own way to Belgian universities.

In the years between 1850 and 1875 there were also closer relations between the two reigning dynasties, with exchanges of gifts and courtesy visits. Between 1854 and 1863, for instance, the Belgian crown prince—later the autocratic Leopold II—travelled extensively in the Ottoman Empire and in Egypt on three separate occasions. In 1860 he visited the Ottoman metropolis, where he met Sultan Abdülmecid. Sultan Abdülaziz's brief 1867 visit to the young kingdom of Belgium during his famous tour of Europe was spectacular as well. Not only was it the first time an Ottoman sovereign had made an official visit to Western Europe, but it was also the first time that a non-European monarch had visited Belgium.

Another mission illustrates Belgium's special place in the thinking of Ottoman statesmen. In the spring of 1871, Istanbul sent Mehmed Kâmil Bey, the Ottoman court's master of ceremonies, to Brussels to deliver the Grand Ribbon of the Osmânî Order to Leopold II. Kâmil Bey's mission was not purely a matter of diplomatic formality but also an occasion to collect economic information. To this purpose he visited factories in Charleroi, including the Solvay company, which would soon be world famous for its new method of producing sodium carbonate.

Friendly Relations

Belgian economic interests in Ottoman territory peaked after 1880. Commercial relations became particularly intense at the turn of the century, and increasing amounts of Belgian capital flowed into the Empire. That was particularly evident in the construction of public utilities such as tramways, water and gas supplies, and later electricity too, in major cities like Izmir (Smyrna), Beirut, and Damascus. In fin-de-siècle Constantinople, Belgian financiers had a virtual monopoly on street lighting via companies such as Gaz de Scutari and Gaz de Stamboul. There were four other Belgian companies in the capital, and at least fourteen in other parts of the empire. In Selânik (present-day Thessaloniki), too, Belgian capitalists had acquired a monopoly on the laying of tramways and of gas and water infrastructure. Members of the Ottoman elites were closely involved in these enterprises. In Salonika, as Western Europeans then called Thessaloniki, one such individual was the energetic mayor and landowner Ahmed Hamdi Bey. Furthermore, Belgian steel foundries and machine builders played significant roles as sub-contractors in the construction of railways in Anatolia, Syria, and the Arabian Peninsula, great infrastructure projects that were a symbol of the characteristic belief in progress and modernity of the time. In 1900 Belgium's exceptional position in the Ottoman economy acquired material and symbolic expression when a neoclassical building on the prestigious Sıraselviler Caddesi was bought to accommodate the Royal Legation. It was the Belgian government's first purchase of that kind.

Stefanaki Karatodori Efendi was better known in Belgium by the French version of his name, Étienne Carathéodory, c. 1885. Signed studio portrait by a Brussels photographer.

The acquisition of what would later come to be called the 'Palais de Belgique' shows the good relations between policymakers in Brussels and Istanbul. Shared economic interests transcended the great differences between the two countries. At times Belgium even pursued a proactive policy towards Istanbul. One example occurred in 1897, when the government took the drastic step of deporting from its national territory the Ottoman intellectual and dissident Ahmed Rıza, the popular European figurehead of the Young Turk movement in Europe. Deaf ears were turned to the outcry from both public and parliament. Such strategic measures ensured that the few diplomatic conflicts that did arise never escalated. This was the case, for instance, during the Joris Affair of 1905–7, when a native of Antwerp who had been living in Istanbul was arrested for complicity in a failed attempt on Sultan Abdülhamid II's life that had been planned by Armenian revolutionaries.

Belgium's official position with regard to the Ottomans was a sharp contrast to those of other European powers, wrapped up as they were in a complex geopolitical competition for spheres of influence. Yet even Belgium played an ambiguous role in the Ottoman Empire. On the one hand, as a political ally, an investor, and a supplier of industrial and military products it indirectly contributed to consolidating Ottoman sovereignty. On the other, Belgian involvement in establishing enterprises and institutions controlled by foreign interests contributed to the Ottomans' increasing dependence on European capital. In that sense, Belgium was part of the 'Western question' confronting the Ottoman ruling class.

Sympathies at the level of high diplomacy were mirrored in friendly contacts between members of the upper classes from both societies. Belgians and Ottomans went hunting together, dined at one another's homes, and intermarried. The most striking example is the diplomat Stefanaki Karatodori Efendi, who for quarter of a century was the Ottoman sultan's representative in Brussels. Karatodori maintained friendly contacts with the highest Belgian officials, government ministers, and even Leopold II himself. He was lionised at the salons and balls of Brussels high society. After his resignation in 1900 he continued to live in his 'second homeland' until his death. The example of Karatodori illustrates how great the similarities were between the elites of the Kingdom of Belgium and the Ottoman Empire. Their exclusive milieu was characterised not only by a shared political conservatism and belief in hierarchical society but also by a relative openness to cultural, confessional, and linguistic diversity. It was a world that the First World War would largely sweep away.

Migration and Tourism

Belgian-Ottoman contacts cannot be defined only in terms of investment, high-level diplomacy, and the social exchanges of the upper crust. Any number of 'ordinary' people migrated in either direction to make Belgium or the Ottoman Empire their temporary or permanent home. We know, for example, that small communities of Sephardic Jews and Armenians from Ottoman territories settled in Antwerp. And while Belgian émigrés were a rarer sight in Ottoman ports, diplomats estimated they totalled two hundred in fin-de-siècle Istanbul.

More and more Belgians also found their way to the Ottoman Empire as tourists. Some could afford the luxury of the Orient Express, which would carry them from Paris to Istanbul in less than three days. Others, like Cyrille Van Overbergh, a Catholic functionary from Kortrijk, went on a Mediterranean cruise. Van Overbergh compiled a hefty record of his journey. Still others took a steamer from Marseille or Trieste for a pilgrimage to the

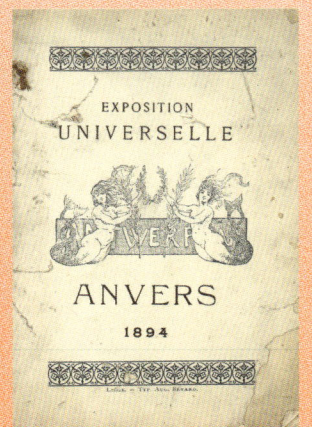 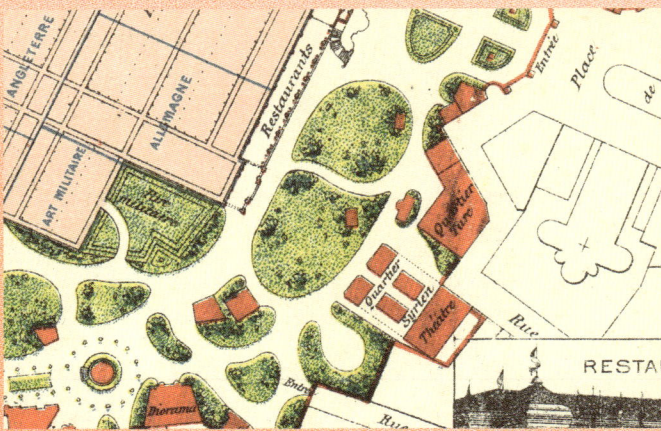

From the brochure for the 1894 World Fair in Antwerp: Ottoman merchants sold their wares in the 'Quartier turc' and 'Quartier syrien', located opposite the German pavilion.

Holy Land, perhaps combined with stop-offs in Egypt and Constantinople. Some, such as the eccentric vegetarian Paul Houyoux and his daughter, a medical student, travelled on a much smaller budget. In 1906 they made their way from Brussels to Antwerp, where they boarded a Deutsche Levant ocean liner for Athens and Istanbul. Their journey illustrates how travelling was becoming much easier and cheaper, but also much more homogenised. Father and daughter Houyoux left with a few clothes in a suitcase and a guidebook in hand. They lamented how easy the journey was and yearned for something more adventurous while sticking to a rigid schedule. Not a single highlight could be missed. In Houyoux senior's words: 'Everything must be seen, and we acquit ourselves of the task methodically.'

To a lesser extent, Ottomans also travelled for pleasure to destinations such as Brussels and Ostend. In 1897 the Ottoman physician and intellectual Şerefeddin Mağmûmî visited the Belgian capital. He was living in Paris, where he was one of the leaders of the Young Turks, opposing Abdülhamid II's regime from exile. He called Brussels 'little Paris' and was especially impressed by the Grand Place and the monumental Palais de Justice. Mağmûmî was there to visit the World Exhibition, where the Ottoman Empire also had a display. The 1897 exhibition attracted over six million visitors, and mass events such as these were the way that most Belgians first encountered the Ottoman Empire, albeit a commercialised and heavily exoticized versions of it. At four of the six world exhibitions held in Belgium between 1885 and 1914 visitors were able to admire the products of Ottoman traders.

The Fracture of War

The First World War deeply altered Ottoman-Belgian relations. The two countries fought on opposite sides, although not directly against one another. During the first year of the war, the Belgian government in exile continued to receive detailed intelligence about domestic developments in the Empire through the two Belgian dragomans in Istanbul who had been allowed to remain in the Ottoman capital. This correspondence ended abruptly in December 1915, when both officials were ordered to leave the Empire. Until the end of the war, the Belgian government had no official representation in Istanbul.

To some Belgians, particularly Catholics, the war also ushered in a short-lived 'Eastern' megalomania. In 1914, the French press was already speculating about the post-war future of areas under the control of the dying Ottoman Empire and the sort of role the Allied powers would play in the region. The future of Palestine was a particular bone of contention: Should the territory be placed under international administration, or entrusted to the protection of a neutral power? Belgium soon put itself in the picture. In 1916 and 1917, a number of Belgian financiers and consuls who were active in Egypt, among them the famed Baron Empain, began to lobby the government in exile. Some diplomats waxed quite lyrical. Baron Ludovic Moncheur, plenipotentiary minister in Constantinople until 1914, sought to draw a direct line between King Albert and Godfrey of Bouillon, the first ruler of the Crusader Kingdom of Jerusalem, writing from London in 1918: 'Every Belgian would be happy and proud to see their glorious sovereign as ruler of Jerusalem and, after eight centuries, succeed the leader of the Crusades, who was also a Belgian and the first to be seated on its throne.'

Some were not content with Palestine and hoped for a Belgian mandate over Istanbul or even all Anatolia. Even though most policymakers, and King Albert himself, were much more cautious and less adventurous, the Hymans government took such ideas very seriously: were the Allies to invite Belgium to exercise a mandate over Palestine after the war, such a request would not be rejected. No less a figure

Postcard with a cartoon of Kaiser Wilhelm II and the Ottoman sultan trudging after his German ally, 1915

Painting of Godfrey of Bouillon by Louis Gallait, undated (before 1887). Belgian Senate, Brussels

than Cardinal Mercier engaged in intense lobbying after the war to gain international support for such an outcome. The British however, who had captured Jerusalem in December 1917, decided Palestine's post-war fate in collusion with the French, thus thwarting any daydreams of the Holy Land becoming a Belgian protectorate.

Belgian post-war interest in occupied Ottoman territory can partly be explained by the government's concern to secure reparations for the losses suffered as a result of German occupation. Acquiring an Ottoman mandate territory was seen as one form of rightful compensation. But the same desire for territorial expansion cannot be separated from prevailing colonial views of the non-European world. The claim on Palestine is symptomatic of the self-regard of a state that in 1908 had officially become a colonial power by annexing immense possessions in Central Africa. During the war and in the context of a decaying Ottoman Empire, colonial thinking merged in some minds with romantic nationalist ideas about 'Belgian' history. Some saw the mythical feats of arms performed in largely Muslim lands by 'national' heroes such as the Frankish crusaders Godfrey of Bouillon and Baldwin IX—respectively the first ruler of the kingdom of Jerusalem and the first Latin emperor of Constantinople—as providing the historical warrant for a Belgian claim to the Holy Land.

After the War: New Powers, Changed Circumstances

After the defeat of the Central Powers, Istanbul was occupied by Allied forces. As early as December 1918, Belgium sent an unofficial representative to the city. But in 1925, when Belgium finally decided to dispatch a permanent diplomatic representative, Constantinople was no longer the capital of an empire. Belgium now had to deal with a new and strong Turkish Republic. The former consulates in the Arab provinces of the vanished Ottoman Empire were reopened as delegations to the French and British mandate authorities, who in true colonial fashion had divided the spoils of war between them. Belgian capitalists tried to pick up the pieces of what they had left behind in 1914 and sought, with varying degrees of success, to breathe new life into their enterprises. The conditions in which they had to operate had, however, changed entirely.

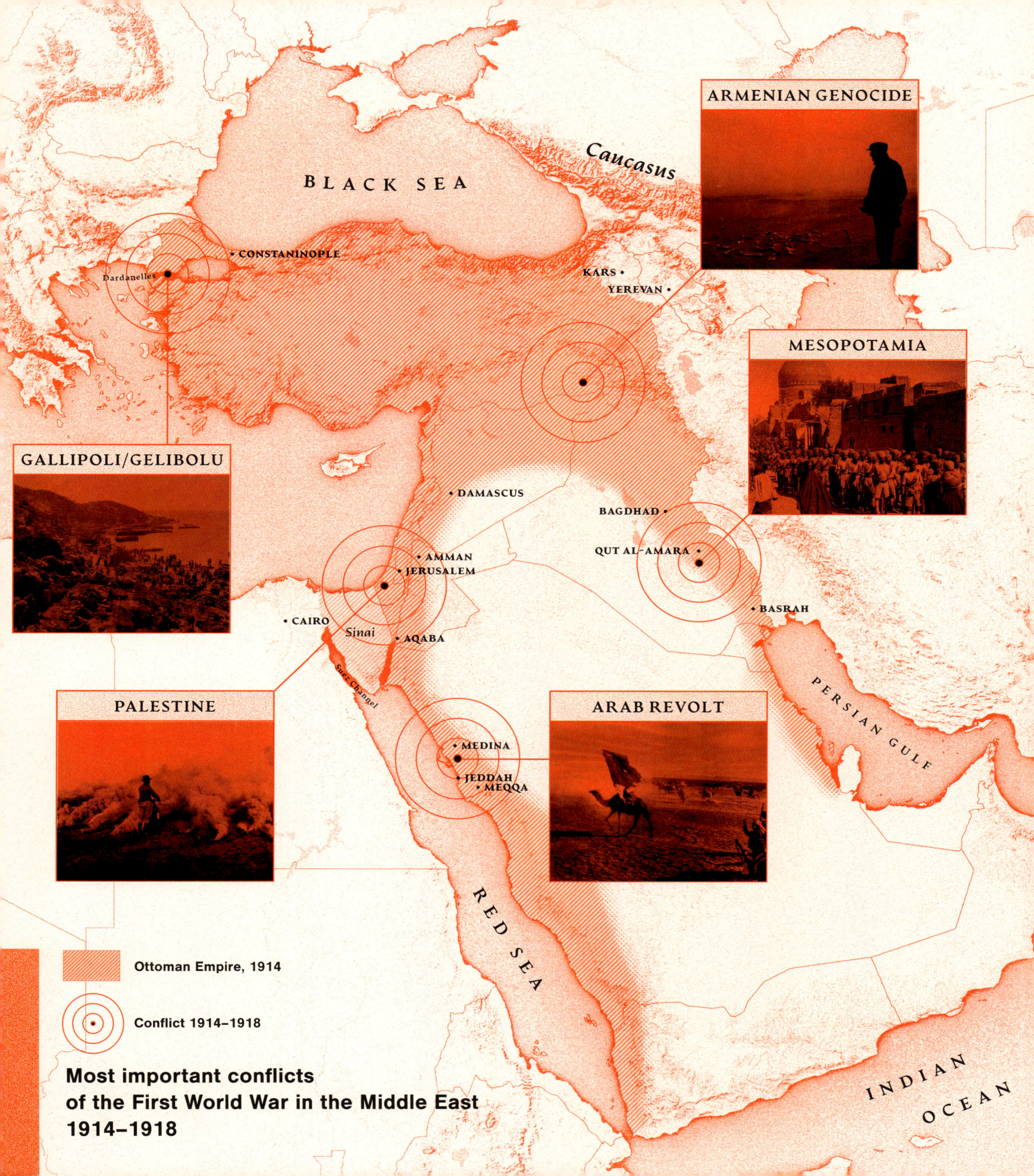

Pieter TROGH

From Declarations of War to Armistice: the First World War in the Middle East, 1914–1918

This essay provides a very brief survey of the course of the First World War in the Middle East between 1914 and 1918. Readers interested in detailed analyses of this period are referred to the reading tips in the bibliography.

1914: Declarations of War and Initial Confrontations

At the end of July 1914, the Ottoman Empire concluded an alliance with Germany. That decision had been helped by events in August 1914. For one thing, the British had confiscated two newly built modern dreadnaughts, ordered and paid for by the Ottoman government with donations from all over the Empire. That gave the Young Turks a useful card to play in the contest for public opinion. For another, at the start of the war Turkey also received the transfer of two German battleships: the *Goeben* and the *Breslau*. That too was part of the reason for eventually choosing Germany. Yet the Ottomans were far from ready for war: they were unprepared militarily, economically, and logistically. The Germans were well aware of that but still hoped to inflict damage on the Allies via the Ottoman Empire. It would be useful if the Muslims in the French and British empires could be inveigled into waging a jihad against their colonial rulers, for instance, or if the Ottomans could threaten some of the British Empire's strategic positions—on the Suez Canal perhaps, or in the Persian Gulf.

Despite the German alliance, the Allies did not declare war on the Ottoman Empire immediately. Among the Young Turks, too, there was initial indecision and discussion. They had no coherent battle plan and were in constant doubt about whether, when, and where they should deploy their troops. To the Germans such vacillation was irritating: the *Goeben*, now renamed the *Yavuz Sultan Selim* but still manned by a German crew, would set a match to the powder keg. In October, therefore, the *Yavuz Sultan Selim* sailed to the Black Sea and shelled Russian ships and positions. That attack led, in early November 1914, to the declaration of war on the Ottoman Empire by Russia, France, and Great Britain.

In November 1914, on behalf of the Ottoman government, the highest religious official in the Ottoman Empire declared jihad, or holy war. This brought the Ottomans some way towards meeting Germany's request to play 'the card of Islam' against Great Britain and France. There were, after all, millions of Muslims in the vast British and French colonial empires. Declaring a holy war should lead to a global Muslim uprising that would destabilise those empires, or so it was believed in Germany. From the

Ottoman unit manning machine guns

start, the Ottoman regime was sceptical about the success of this tactic. It was a sensitive issue. There was great religious and ethnic diversity among the subjects of their own empire. One wrong word could produce the completely opposite effect. In spite of a frenetic propaganda campaign, 'the German-made jihad' came to nothing. Even so, well into the war, the British in particular were still afraid that Muslims would revolt in their colonies of Egypt, Sudan, and India. In that sense, the threat of a jihad had a greater effect than if it had actually happened.

Meanwhile, the Young Turks were also becoming increasingly determined to launch offensives against the Allies. In December 1914, an overconfident Enver Pasha sent in the Ottoman Third Army against the Russian positions in the Caucasus. The momentarily panicked Russians asked the British to attack elsewhere in the Middle East and thus divert attention, but in the event they inflicted a crushing defeat on the Ottomans themselves. Of the 100,000 or so Ottoman servicemen who fought in the harsh winter conditions in the Caucasus, only 30% returned. Despite that disaster, Enver Pasha immediately ordered a second offensive, this time against the British entrenched on the Suez Canal. It was yet another ill-prepared campaign, resulting in early February 1915 in yet another debacle. But at least the Ottomans, assisted by German officers, had shown the British that they could strike at them in a strategic location.

1915: Escalation

Although the Russians had the situation in the Caucasus under control, the British nevertheless decided to go ahead with their request to open a front elsewhere. Their eye fell on the strategic Dardanelles, which gave access to Constantinople, the Ottoman capital. Inside the British admiralty there were heated discussions about how to force a passage through the strait: Should it be by ship only, or by a combined action of ships and infantry landings? Since Herbert Kitchener, the British Commander-in-Chief, was reluctant to release units of the already decimated British Army on the Western Front, there was really only one alternative—it would have to be 'ships alone' for the Dardanelles. On 18 March 1915, British and French warships attempted to force the strait—and failed. Nonetheless, the British—with Winston Churchill the most vocal among supporters of the plan—were unwilling to give up the Dardanelles just yet. Troops were eventually found for a combined action—a British reserve division, several French units, and men from the dominions, mostly Australians and New Zealanders, who had just arrived in Egypt.

On 25 April, Allied ground forces landed on the Gallipoli Peninsula (Gelibolu in Turkish). The campaign was not well prepared: too little was known about the terrain, communications were defective, and there was insufficient artillery support for the landing troops. Moreover, the Ottomans mounted a stubborn defence, their artillery and snipers causing many casualties among the Allied attackers. The situation at Gallipoli soon turned into a stalemate. Fresh assaults in the course of May and June 1915 came to nothing. But neither were the Ottomans able to drive the Allies from the peninsula. Brutal trench warfare was the result. As summer wore on, the pitiless heat and the lack of drinking water affected the men on both sides. In August 1915 another landing was attempted, at Suvla Bay: that too was a failure. Finally, in the winter of 1915–1916, the Allied troops were evacuated. Gallipoli had taken a toll of over 44,000 dead and almost 100,000 wounded. Ottoman losses were also substantial—in the course of the campaign an estimated 78,000 were killed and 167,000 fell sick or were wounded. But for the Ottomans their victory at Gallipoli had great symbolic importance. It had shown that they could defeat the Allies. A pivotal figure in that success was the Ottoman

Left: A British soldier offers his flask to an Ottoman prisoner of war, Gallipoli, 1915

Right: ANZAC soldiers look at the casualties who fell by their trenches, Lone Pine, August 1915

commander Mustafa Kemal. At Gallipoli the foundation was laid for his later mythical status.

While fierce fighting was still going on in Gallipoli, a tragedy of unprecedented proportions was taking place in the interior of the Ottoman Empire: the Armenian Genocide. There were several reasons for the Young Turk regime's decision to proceed with the destruction of the empire's Armenian population. There was, for instance, a general frustration at the loss of territory—and of face—in the previous decades, the trauma of the massacres of Muslims during the Balkan Wars (1912–1913), the subsequent streams of refugees heading for Anatolia, the fear of Armenian nationalism, and the incremental increase of foreign interference in the Ottoman Empire's internal affairs. The First World War acted as a catalyst. The military defeats in the Caucasus and the Suez Canal demanded a scapegoat, and when the Allies arrived at Gallipoli, the Young Turks panicked. That they chose this moment to get rid of the Armenians once and for all is not a coincidence.

It began during the night of 24 April 1915 in Constantinople: 250 Armenian intellectuals, artists, politicians, writers, and businessmen were dragged from their beds and arrested. They were taken inland and executed. From May 1915, the Armenian population (some one and a half million people), who lived mainly in the central and eastern parts of what is now Turkey, were rounded up and deported. Often the men were first separated and killed. Women, children, and the elderly were forced to make their way on foot to the Syrian desert, a thousand kilometres away. Hundreds of thousands perished on those death marches. The survivors were dispersed into concentration camps, where they received hardly any food and where thousands more died. Another strategy for the elimination of Armenians from society was the forced conversion of the survivors. Women were married off to Muslims; orphans were placed in Muslim families. In addition, Armenian built heritage, such as churches and monasteries, was razed.

The Armenian Genocide was a large-scale phenomenon involving many different dimensions and aspects. Thus, it was more than 'a mass murder'. In total, at least 900,000 Armenians lost their lives. That genocide surpassed every other form of repressive or ethnic violence during the First World War. The Young Turk regime also dealt very harshly with other groups in the Empire, such as Arab nationalists (1915–1916) and Assyrian Christians (1915).

1916

When it was finally apparent that Gallipoli was a disaster, London agreed to launch a new campaign in Mesopotamia. The British needed a success to avoid losing face. In the autumn of 1915, they advanced rapidly along the Tigris and by early December had reached Baghdad. There, the offensive stalled and they fell back to Kut al-Amara. At the end of April 1916, after a long siege by the Ottoman army and several failed attempts to relieve the city, the British surrendered Kut to the Ottomans.

In turn, the Ottomans prepared a daring new campaign across the Sinai desert. In the summer of 1916, the British were alarmed to discover that a German-led Ottoman force was less than fifty kilometres from the Suez Canal. After a few short but hard-fought battles the Allies managed to push the Ottomans back from the Sinai desert, but the new threat had made them realise that if the Suez Canal was to be permanently secured, the 'defensive zone' would have to be extended to Palestine. And that meant that the desert would have to be 'tamed'. Over the course of 1916 and early 1917, 354 kilometres of asphalt road, 578 kilometres of railway, and 483 kilometres of water pipeline were laid through the Sinai desert. Soldiers did much of the heavy

An Australian 'cavalryman' of the Imperial Camel Corps

lifting, but their efforts were supported by the forced labour of thousands of native workers.

1916 was also a pivotal year for behind-the-scenes geopolitics. The campaigns at Gallipoli and in Mesopotamia had left the British in no doubt that to win war in the Middle East they would need an additional ally. That ally they found in the Hejaz region, where the Hashemite house of Hussein ibn Ali, the Sharif of Mecca, had long been hostile to the Ottoman regime. In return for a post-war independent Arab state led by Hussein, he and his son, Prince Faisal, would initiate an Arab revolt behind Ottoman lines. The new state would encompass the entire Arabian Peninsula plus Syria, Jordan, Lebanon, Palestine, and Iraq. Although only part of the Arab population within the Ottoman Empire harboured Arab nationalist ambitions, Sharif Hussein's clan assured the Allies that he spoke for all Arabs. Between July 1915 and January 1916, Hussein and Arthur McMahon, the British High Commissioner to Egypt, exchanged letters on the matter. The British agreed, and accordingly, in June 1916, the Arab revolt began. Just a few months earlier, however, talks between the British and French had also started, with assent from the Russians and Italians, to discuss the partition of the Ottoman Empire into British and French spheres of influence. The results of those negotiations were set out in the secret Sykes-Picot treaty. But then, in 1917, the British issued a statement, known as the Balfour Declaration, announcing their support for the establishment of a Jewish homeland in Palestine. That was obviously irreconcilable with British promises previously made to the Arab nationalists.

1917–1918

In 1917, the war in the Middle East was being fought on three main fronts: Mesopotamia, southern Palestine, and the Hejaz region. By 1916, the Russians had pushed back the Ottomans on the Caucasus front between Trabzon and Lake Van and subsequently that front remained relatively stable. The Ottomans now had too few forces to mount major offensives themselves and mainly tried to stand their ground. The initiative lay with the Allies. By January 1917 they had built up a new force to deploy in Mesopotamia. First, Indian troops captured Kut al-Amara and on 9 March they took Baghdad, where they halted for a time.

Meanwhile, the Allies had also built a logistical bridge across the Sinai Desert, and in March 1917 they arrived at Gaza. Their first attack failed; a second attempt in April 1917 was also repulsed by the Ottoman defence. In the summer, General Edmund Allenby arrived to take command of the Egyptian Expeditionary Force (EEF). He created a new dynamic: at the end of October 1917, his troops broke through the Ottoman defences: on 9 December Jerusalem was captured. It was a welcome victory for the British Empire after the disastrous Third Battle of Ypres. But hopes of a further British advance were hindered by the German spring offensives in 1918 on the Western Front.

With the campaigns in Palestine and in Mesopotamia at an impasse, the main threat to the Ottomans now came from the Arab tribal federations in the Hejaz region. The Arab Revolt had got off to a slow start in the summer of 1916, but with British and French support in the form of money, weapons

Left: British Indian troops receive their orders during the Mesopotamia campaign, 1917

Right: The Arab Revolt. Troops of Prince Faisal advance towards Wejh, January 1917

and several units it began to pick up pace the following year. In popular culture, T. E. Lawrence—the famous Lawrence of Arabia—has become the figurehead of the revolt, but in reality many others contributed to it. Arab troops first attacked along the coast of what is today Saudi Arabia. Supported by British naval forces, they captured a number of strategic ports such as Jeddah and Aqaba. In 1917 and 1918, the Arab rebels also waged a kind of guerrilla war along the Hejaz Railway and made things quite difficult for the Ottomans.

At the end of September 1918, the decisive phase that would end the First World War began. On the Macedonian front, Allied troops forced Bulgaria (allied with the Central Powers) to its knees. In Europe, the Germans were pushed back all along the Western Front. And in the Middle East, a combination of Arab raids behind Ottoman lines and superior Allied military power in Palestine led to the capture of Damascus and Aleppo in October 1918. On 31 October the Armistice of Mudros was signed, ending hostilities between the Ottomans and the Allies: the Ottoman Empire ceased to exist.

In late 1914, few would have predicted that the Ottoman Empire—labelled by the West 'the sick man of Europe'—would hold out for four years. Between the end of October 1914 and the end of October 1918, an estimated two and a half million Ottoman citizens (more than 10% of the total population of the Ottoman Empire in 1914) had died: one and a half million had succumbed to disease, epidemics, and famine, and almost one million Armenians had been exterminated in the genocide. In addition, an estimated 800,000 Ottoman soldiers were also killed. On the Allied side, the Commonwealth numbered about 122,000 and the French nearly 10,000 dead. On the Russian side, the number of casualties on the Caucasus front is estimated at 140,000.

Although the French and British had not necessarily wanted war with the Ottoman Empire, they had nevertheless become involved in it through a series of events. The war in the Middle East started slowly but grew in importance as the conflict progressed. Due to the increasing involvement of allied troops—particularly from the British Commonwealth—ambitions with regard to the post-war partition of the Ottoman Empire also grew. Various local communities had hopes of finally achieving self-government and autonomy, and other groups had also received promises during the war. Between the end of 1918 and 1923, an extremely important historical period began for the future of the Middle East.

Falih RIFKI

1894–1971

Falih Rıfkı was a promising journalist who began his career at *Tanin*, the official newspaper of the Committee for Unity and Progress (CUP), the party of the Young Turks. When war broke out, Rıfkı, then in his twenties, became a reserve officer in the Ottoman army. His fluent pen soon caught the attention of the leaders of the Young Turks, and before long he was appointed personal secretary to Talaat Pasha, the minister of the interior. In February 1915, he was transferred to Syria, where he became aide-de-camp to Governor-General Djemal Pasha. As Djemal's closest associate, he was an important eyewitness to policy in the region. Rıfkı accompanied his chief everywhere. He recalled a festive evening in Lebanon to which Djemal Pasha and his aide were invited. The abundance of food at the banquet was in sharp contrast to the great famine that reigned 'out there'. As he looked at the heavily spiced Syrian buffet and the wide range of drinks, including fine Rhenish wines, Falih suddenly felt a lump in his throat as sounds from the world outside penetrated through the window:

> 'A deep wave of pitiful wailing sound was coming toward us like the haunting echoes from a deep well. The whole street is moaning. We were hearing the moans of those in their death throes from hunger, those walking skeletons who were crawling toward us on the street. A refuse cart passed by us; I saw an arm dangling out. The municipality was collecting the dead and the nearly dead. It was necessary to silence the streets before dawn. The sweepers of ordure and death are completing the sad morning toilette of Beirut. I wanted to vomit all I had drunk, women's laughter, electricity, the whole of Beirut, and the war. Like the murderer of those about to die, I froze, expecting at any moment, from any quarter, the arm that would seize me. When I went to bed that night, I tried to reduce my pain by pressing my fist into my stomach. That dawn in Beirut I saw the real face of war.'

Rıfkı's memoirs were first published in 1932. After the war, he became an ardent follower of Mustafa Kemal Atatürk. Between 1923 and 1950, he was a member of the Turkish parliament.

Portrait of a young Falih Rıfkı

Djemal Pasha and his entourage; Falih Rıfkı is on the far right

Destroyed British tank during the Second Battle of Gaza, April 1917. Falih Rıfkı wrote in his journal: 'We are now fighting in Gaza on the Palestine front. An English tank, not finding anybody to kill on either side, has become a metal skeleton, baking in the Palestinian sun.'

Falih Rıfkı

Men of the Egyptian Labour Corps at work in Boulogne-sur-Mer. Many of them also worked behind the Allied lines at De Panne and Adinkerke.

Pieter TROGH

Wavell's Eye: Connections between Flanders Fields and the Middle East in the First World War

In the aftermath of the Paris Peace Conference in 1919, the British Brigadier General Archibald Wavell voiced his dissatisfaction at the outcome of the peace treaties. He put it thus: 'After "the war to end war" they seem to have been pretty successful in Paris at making a "Peace to end Peace".' Wavell's comment referenced the title of a book by H. G. Wells, *The War That Will End War*. Published in 1914, it had quickly become a common catchphrase. Wavell's version is known chiefly through being picked up—and slightly modified—decades later by the American historian David Fromkin for his 1989 book *A Peace to End All Peace*, an often-cited analysis of the fall of the Ottoman Empire and the creation of the modern Middle East.

When Wavell made his remark he had only one eye, having lost the other to artillery shrapnel during the Second Battle of Ypres (22 April–24 May 1915) while serving as a staff officer in the Ypres Salient. He carried the scar for the rest of his life, also when he was transferred to Palestine to join the staff of General Edmund Allenby, commander of the Egyptian Expeditionary Force (EEF). Although there is no causal connection between the eye he lost at Ypres and his animadversions on the pernicious peace settlements of the First World War, Flanders Fields and the Middle East are inextricably linked through the figure of Archibald Wavell.

Seen through the prism of war, thousands of connections can thus be brought to light between *In Flanders Fields*—as a metaphor for the front in Flanders—and the Middle East. Sometimes that connection touched on the highest levels of strategic decision-making, from which it appears that, through the years of conflict, those two theatres of war sometimes acted like communicating vessels. Winston Churchill is one example. In early 1915, then First Lord of the Admiralty, his was one of the loudest voices arguing in favour of forcing a passage through the strategic Dardanelles to defeat the Ottoman Empire. A naval bombardment on 18 March and landings combined with naval gunfire on 25 April 1915 both ended in disastrous failure. Churchill—who happened to be visiting the Ypres Salient on the day before the landings—was made the scapegoat for the Gallipoli fiasco and was forced to resign from the government. He also imposed a penance on himself: six months' 'service at the front'. From December 1915 to April 1916 Churchill was the battalion commander of a unit at Ploegsteert, one of the quietest sectors of the Flanders front.

Sir Archibald Wavell

Percy Clark of the Australian 11th Infantry Battalion posed with the entire battalion at the Pyramid of Giza in January 1915 (see photograph on pp. 68–69). He survived the Gallipoli campaign in 1915 but was killed in action at Zonnebeke on 30 October 1917.

Usually, however, the connection runs through the trail of soldiers who swapped the sand of the desert for the mud of Flanders, or vice versa. Most were British Commonwealth servicemen—not in itself surprising given how many fought on both the Western Front and in the Middle East. As far as we know, none of the French, German, or Austro-Hungarian troops who fought in the Middle East also served in Flanders Fields. Nor did Ottoman units or individuals reach the Flanders front. If we were to interpret the Middle East as the 'Islamic world', the connection with Flanders Fields would be greater and more diverse. Think of the *tirailleurs*, Zouaves, and spahis that France deployed from its colonies of Algeria, Tunisia, and Morocco. At least 3300 of them fell in Flanders Fields. But as this book focuses on the fronts in the Ottoman Empire—particularly the present-day countries of Egypt, Lebanon, Iraq, Syria, Israel/Palestine, Turkey, Jordan, and Saudi Arabia—those troops are not mentioned in its pages.

Communicating Vessels

During the First World War, fighting took place in different parts of the world. The leaders of the belligerent parties constantly had to decide on the approach to each battle front. Operational strategies were determined by personal convictions, war objectives, available resources (logistics and manpower), the course of the campaign, opportunities, winning or losing battles. War fronts were never isolated cases but functioned as communicating vessels. Likewise, in Flanders Fields and the Middle East.

The first British attempt to force the Dardanelles, on 18 March 1915, was made by ships alone. There was considerable scepticism within the British Admiralty as to whether such an action could succeed without the support of an infantry landing. But at the time there were simply no troops available. The British Commander-in-Chief, Herbert Kitchener, had no desire to redeploy troops from the Western Front—it was only a matter of months since the professional British army had been decimated at the First Battle of Ypres. A propaganda campaign was underway to recruit hundreds of thousands of volunteers for a new British army, but it took time to mobilise and deploy. After the failure of the 'ships alone' scenario, the British had to wait for a British reserve division, several French units, and troops from the dominions of Australia and New Zealand who had just arrived in Egypt, before a landing at Gallipoli could be mounted.

At the end of 1916 there was a change of government in Britain and David Lloyd George became Prime Minister. Consequently, the importance of the Middle East to Britain's war strategy greatly increased, for Lloyd George saw more likelihood of the First World War being won 'in the East' than on the Western Front, where everything was deadlocked. The Flanders offensive (31 July–12 November 1917) only reinforced that belief. The Third Battle of Ypres ended in the mud of Passchendaele after more than a hundred days and an advance of a mere eight kilometres to a target that should have been captured on the second day. For Lloyd George, the Flanders debacle was a potential disgrace. He was in dire need of a triumph of some kind. He gave Allenby the troops that were needed to break through Gaza and capture Jerusalem. 'Jerusalem before Christmas', Lloyd George promised the press. And that promise was kept: on 9 December 1917, Jerusalem surrendered to British troops.

In 1918 Allenby proposed a further advance through Palestine to deal a final blow to the Ottoman Empire, but events on the Western Front decreed otherwise. On 21 March 1918 the Germans, having defeated Tsarist Russia, launched a major offensive in a final attempt to achieve victory on the Western Front. The German spring offensive, which was launched in France but later struck north into Flanders, took the Allies by surprise. The Germans made

Winston Churchill as battalion commander of the 6th Bn. Royal Scots Fusiliers, somewhere behind the front at Ploegsteert, early 1916

deep gains in territory, which caused panic. Several of Allenby's divisions were withdrawn and rushed westward to hold the Allied line there. That change of direction had such a great impact that any further progress in the Palestine offensive had to be postponed until September 1918. Then, as was also happening on the Western Front, the Allies achieved major successes in the Middle East, which culminated in an armistice.

Between Flanders Fields and the Middle East

The British soldier George Knox died near Kut al-Amara (Iraq) on 9 April 1916. As his body was never recovered, his name was carved on a monument to the missing after the war. Because the British War Graves Commission had lost track of Knox in an administrative mix up, his name did not appear on the Basra Memorial in Iraq, but by mistake on the Menin Gate in Ypres. The connections between Flanders Fields and the Middle East ran in various ways through the lives and war experiences of thousands of soldiers: through their pre-war professions, a family tie, through exchanging one front for another, through origin or simply through coincidence, as in the case of George Knox. Some examples follow.

In mid-November 1914, the French Colonel Gaston Cros arrived with the 2nd Moroccan Brigade at the front at Ypres to face the German armies. It was a bloodbath that cost the lives of many of Cros's North African *tirailleurs* and Zouaves. As far as we know, Cros did not keep a diary so we have no insight into his state of mind during those days and can only wonder whether he recalled better times when he dug into the earth. Cros was an amateur archaeologist. Between 1901 and 1912, he led a French military-archaeological expedition to excavate the ancient Sumerian site at Girsu (Iraq). The Tello expedition, as it was called, yielded thousands of artefacts and figurines from the Sumer civilisation, which were earnestly 'rehoused' in the Louvre in Paris. Cros was one of dozens of archaeologists who later took part in the First World War. At present he is the only known archaeologist with a link in Flanders.

The family relationships that link both fronts are more numerous. General Edmund Allenby had just arrived in Palestine when word reached him that his son, Horace Allenby, a lieutenant in the Royal Horse Artillery, had been killed at Koksijde on 29 July 1917. Today, Horace still lies in Coxyde Military Cemetery. There are also many instances of a pair of brothers dying, one in Flanders Fields, the other in the Middle East. One example: the moving plight of at least three sets of parents who were unable to visit the graves of their sons after the war, as none of the bodies were ever found. The brothers' names are commemorated on the Menin Gate in Ypres and the Basra Memorial in Iraq, respectively: John (d. 18/4/1915) and George Morgan (d. 22/4/1916); Ernest Edwin (d. 23/4/1915) and John Alfred Rout (d. 28/9/1915); Rupert George (d. 24/5/1915) and Frederick Cecil Boosey (d. 22/11/1915).

The largest group linking the two fronts were the thousands of soldiers who exchanged the Middle East for Flanders Fields, or vice versa: from entire divisions to reorganised units; from Indian troops who did not do well in the climate of Flanders and were sent to Mesopotamia to the thousands of Gallipoli veterans who later died at Ypres; from well-known war poets like Francis Ledwidge or generals like Allenby and the Frenchman Franchet d'Esperey to noble unknowns.

Also notable were several companies of the Egyptian Labour Corps (ELC), which was created to meet the general shortage of cheap manpower that made Allied warfare in the Middle East logistically possible. Tens of thousands of Egyptian workers were deployed to bypass the Sinai desert. They laid hundreds of kilometres of railways, roads, and water pipelines. Their fate was pitiable. They suffered racial

Men of the Egyptian Labour Corps en route to northern France. Many of them also worked behind the Allied lines at De Panne and Adinkerke.

abuse and regularly received harsh corporal punishment. A British conscientious objector in Egypt observed:

> 'The treatment of these Egyptians is a scandal. They talk about modern civilisation and abolishing slavery, yet these men have taskmasters paid by the British government to whip them like dogs with long leather whips. Even the British and the Australians kick and bully them unmercifully. Let us take the beam from our eyes before talking about Germany and her allies.'

In the spring of 1917, in preparation for the Third Battle of Ypres, Egyptian (and Chinese and South African) labour corps were sent to northern France to do the heavy and dirty work behind the Allied lines. They too suffered casualties: from illness, deprivation, or, when they worked within range of German artillery, from bursting shells. In Flanders a single fatality is a reminder of their presence: Sabit Harun Mohamed died on 6 September 1917 and is commemorated at Adinkerke Military Cemetery. Dozens of his comrades are buried a little further away, along the Opal Coast.

Finally, we also find 'traces' of the Middle East on British trench maps from the Westhoek. Staff officers of the cartographic service devised toponyms for the maps, which were intended to help soldiers orientate themselves in the topographies of the front. The place names could refer to recognisable features in the landscape (such as Graveyard Cottage) but there were also allusions to home (such as Tyne Cot, the term for a typical cottage on the River Tyne), or to military events (Zouave Wood, for example) or individuals (Plumer Trench), or other fronts. On the Westhoek trench maps there are numerous toponyms that reference the Middle East: Baghdad Siding, Bedouin Trench, Cairo House Post, Camel Drive, Gallipoli Copse and Farm, Jaffa Road, Jericho Street, Jerusalem Farms, Lemnos House, Orient Avenue, Palestine Bridge, Palestine Trench, Suez Farm Post...

War Experience

War experience in the Middle East could hardly have been more different from its equivalent in Flanders Fields (and the Western Front). With its muddy trenches, barbed wire, daily shelling, major offensives, and 'minor operations', the front in Flanders was reputed to be one of the worst war zones a soldier could end up in. Death lurked just around the corner, each and every day, even in 'calmer' periods. In the Middle East, the threats from industrial weapons of mass destruction were less constantly present, although according to eyewitnesses who had seen action on both fronts, the intensity of some battles (such as Ctesiphon in November 1915, or Gaza in April 1917) was certainly on a level with the Western Front. The Middle East war experience became notorious for daily hardships of a different nature: the scorching sun, the sand that got in everywhere, and the vermin that carried potentially fatal diseases such as malaria and sandfly fever. But it was mostly the exposure to the unforgiving climate that affected the men so badly: hundreds died as a direct result of the searing temperature—from sunstroke, dehydration, heart attack. Unrelenting heat and the constant thirst that went with it could physically and emotionally crush the most hardened man every bit as much as minutes-long artillery barrages on the Western Front.

Psychologically, two other factors posed a severe test for soldiers in the Middle East. The first was akin to homesickness. In the Middle East, the Commonwealth servicemen found themselves in a world very different from the one they had left. They missed the familiarity of something that seemed like 'home', such as the estaminets and western customs that they did encounter behind the front in Flanders. Letters from loved ones at home took much longer to reach the Middle East front, and for the men 'out East' there was no question of a few days' home leave. Secondly, the absence of clear military objectives in the Middle East created feelings of inadequacy and

Australian and British soldiers in a trench at Gallipoli

disappointment in the men who fought there. On the Western Front, the battle to liberate Belgium and northern France was a clear and straightforward aim for as long as it was not achieved. In the Middle East, exactly what was being fought for was much less evident, which also left its mark on both the collective and individual memory of war experience there.

Justin Fantauzzo has studied this subject extensively through detailed examination of numerous memoirs and diaries kept by those soldiers. From these it appears that a definite hierarchy had formed between the fronts: those who had fought in the West against Germany had contributed more to the Allied victory than those who saw combat in a 'sideshow' such as the Middle East or Macedonia. That, at least, was the perception of public opinion, which already seeped into the minds of 'the men out East' during the war. In their testimonies, those servicemen struggled to give a meaning to their war experience. Many of them found peace of mind in a narrative that reflected British imperialist thinking: they had waged 'a modern crusade', they had fought 'for the liberation of long oppressed peoples', they had 'brought civilisation' to a world they believed to be deprived and backward. Others consoled themselves with the thought that their struggle was part of a bigger picture, a world war, and therefore had been just as valuable. In discussions or in the public memory, however, the legitimacy of their war experience was often brushed aside. The association of the First World War with scenes of the Western Front still overshadows the memory of other war fronts today.

Frank HURLEY

1885–1962

On 11 October 1917, the Australian photographer Frank Hurley wrote in his diary: 'For there is no place in eternity that is more hellish....' He was referring to Ypres, where he had witnessed the Third Battle of Ypres. Hurley had been sent along with the Australian army to take pictures of the war. Deeply impressed by what he saw at and behind the front, he quickly realised the impossibility of portraying it by means of classical photography. Thus, he began to experiment with new techniques and perspectives, eventually arriving at what he called 'composites', pictures that are made up of several different images—Photoshop before it was invented, as it were. This, thought Hurley, was the only way to represent the war in photographs, the only way that came close to reality. Not everyone agreed. Frank had heated discussions about it with his superiors.

After Ypres, Hurley was sent to Egypt and Palestine, which he reached in mid-December 1917. His aim was 'to take a series of publicity photos' and train the photographers who were already there. He arrived shortly after Jerusalem had been taken and the actual fighting was over. Consequently, he had to have many of the attacks, troop formations, and aeroplane manoeuvres re-enacted for the camera. Close examination of the pictures reveals that Hurley introduced the 'Ypres' techniques and viewpoints in Palestine too: laid side by side, they could almost be mirror images.

Those were the only two fronts that Hurley saw during the First World War. Thus, it seems logical that he would have compared them with each other. On 6 February 1918, he wrote in his diary:

'I had two squadrons sent to Gaza to participate in my pictures. The weather turned out excellent and I did some excellent work ... We wandered all over Gaza, which once must have been a very fine town, but nowhere did I see an intact building, not even a room. Gaza is the Ypres of Palestine ...'

Portrait of Frank Hurley.

'Battle-scarred sentinels.' Remnant of a fine old avenue on the infamous track through Chateau Wood (Zonnebeke), 1917

The minarets of Cairo, December 1917. Egypt was the first stop of Hurley's period in the Middle East.

'Clearing the heights of enemy snipers'. Na'alin, Palestine, 1918
'Going over the top', Zonnebeke, 1917

A flight of bombers, 1st Australian Flying Corps, Palestine, 1918
Shrapnel bursting amongst reconnaissance planes, Ypres front, 1917

An oasis in the desert, Palestine, 1918

The world's most infamous highway. The Menin road by a winter's sunset, 1917

Frank Hurley

49   An Ottoman officer

Ottoman prisoners of war,
presumably at Gallipoli, 1915

Ottoman officers during the First World War

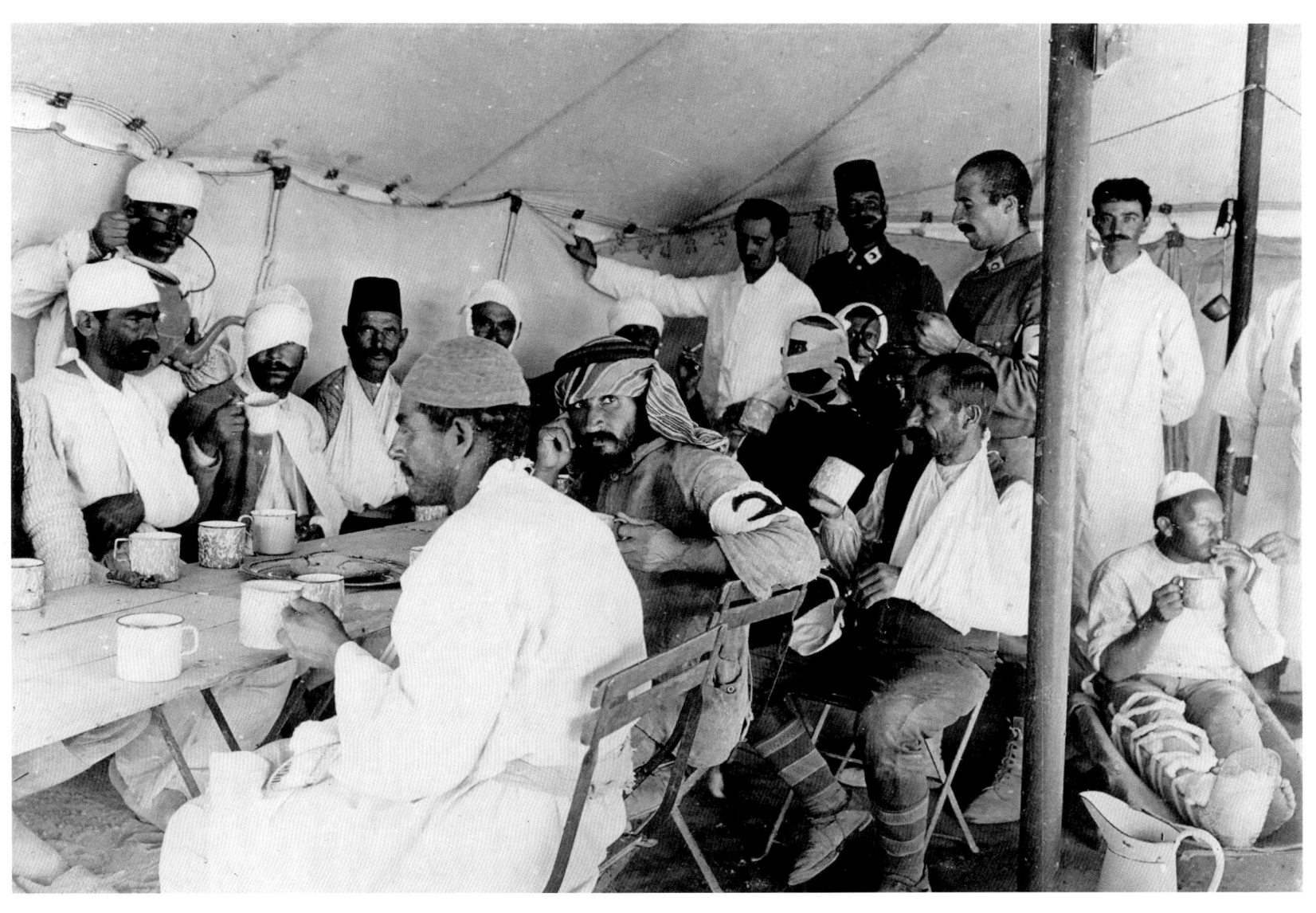

The interior of an Ottoman field hospital tent at Hafir Aujah, Sinai desert, 1916

The Ottoman field hospital at Hafir
Aujah, Sinai desert, 1916

An Ottoman soldier from a medical unit poses next to his camel. In the background is the Ottoman field hospital at Hafir Aujah, Sinai desert, 1916.

Ottoman infantry column at rest

A delegation from the Ottoman parliament is received in Jericho by Djemal Pasha, governor-general of Syria, Lebanon, and Palestine. Djemal Pasha is in the centre of the picture. Also in the photograph is Friedrich Kress von Kressenstein (second from left), the German general who led the Ottoman campaigns through the Sinai desert.

Ottomans killed in a counterattack north of Jerusalem, late December 1917

Memorial cross commemorating men of the British 161st Infantry Brigade, who fell during the First Battle of Gaza, 26 March 1917

Austrian troops leave Jerusalem just before the British take the city in early December 1917. Both Germany and Austria-Hungary, the allies of the Ottoman Empire, sent troops to the Middle East to support the Ottomans.

Indian and British soldiers stand guard at Jerusalem's Jaffa Gate, December 1917

British Colonel Ronald Storrs poses with local dignitaries at the shrine of Nabi (or Nebi) Mousa, a site near Jericho where, according to Islam, the tomb of Moses (Musa) is located.

British soldiers in their trench, Gallipoli, 1915

German and Ottoman wounded are evacuated in lorries, Palestine, 1918

French *Tirailleurs sénégalais* gathering in the port of Mudros (Lemnos) to be disembarked at the Dardanelles, 1915

British artillery in action at Cape Helles, Gallipoli, June 1915

The Imperial Camel Corps going into action, Palestine, 1918.
Photograph by Frank Hurley

Camel transport passing through a flooded wadi during the torrential rains of the wet season, Esdud (Ashdod, Israel), 1918. Photograph by Frank Hurley

A New Zealand soldier experiments with creating a smoke screen, Egypt, 1917

A halt in the desert with the Australian Light Horse, Palestine, 1918. Photograph by Frank Hurley

Group photograph of the Australian 11th Infantry Battalion at the Great Pyramid of Giza in Egypt, January 1915. Research has shown that at least ten of the men in this photograph survived the Gallipoli Campaign but later lost their lives at the Third Battle of Ypres.

Camel transport conveying bales of straw from the railhead to an advanced distribution centre, Ramallah, 1918.
Photograph by Frank Hurley

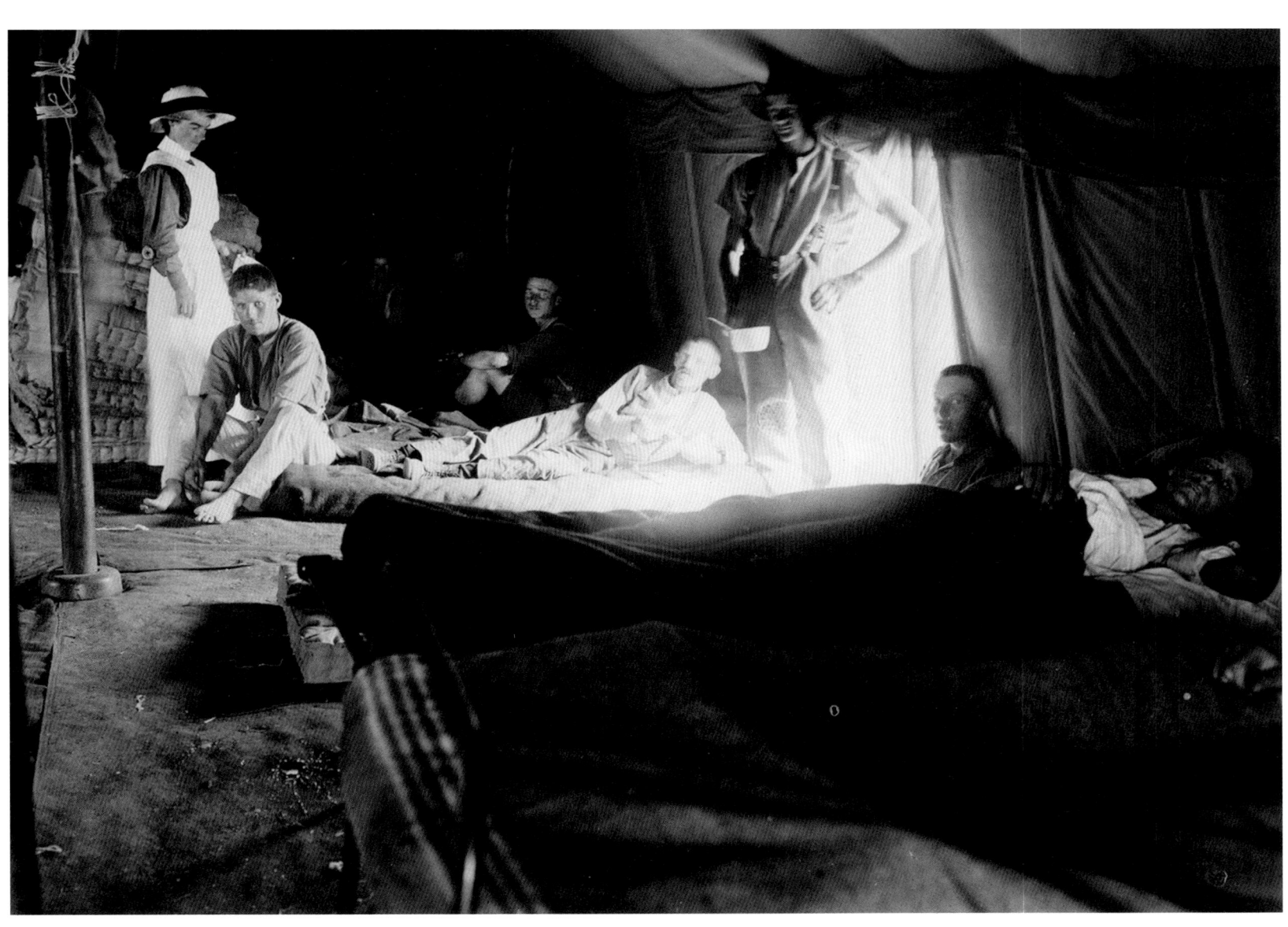

Interior view of a ward at the 3rd Australian General Hospital on Lemnos, late April 1915

Arab tribesmen, 1916

The Arab Revolt. A flag bearer on a camel during the capture of Aqaba, 6 July 1917

Faisal's army camp during the Arab Revolt, 1918

Indian troops during the Mesopotamia (modern Iraq) campaign, 1916. In total, around 1 million Indian troops served in the Middle East during the First World War.

Shenorhig TENGUERIAN

1905 – ?

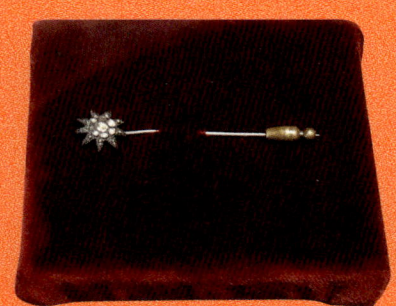

The tiepin of Melkon Tenguerian, which he gave to his daughter as a talisman at the time of his arrest

In April 1915, Melkon Tenguerian, a resident of Sivas, was arrested by Ottoman-Turkish gendarmes for the crime of being Armenian. He had to leave behind his wife and four children. Before he was led away, Melkon put his tiepin in his daughter Shenorhig's hands, as a sort of talisman. Melkon was hanged and a few weeks later his family was deported to the south, along with all the other Armenians from Sivas. During those infamous death marches—one of the tactics the Ottoman regime used to destroy the Armenians—Shenorhig lost two sisters, her brother, and her mother.

By some miracle, Shenorhig herself survived the death march. She ended up with a Kurdish family who tried to convert her to Islam. To that end they even tattooed her face with the crescent moon symbol. Towards the end of the war, Shenorhig was sent to an orphanage, where she was safe. After the war, she emigrated to America but carried her scars with her, literally and figuratively. It was not until the 1970s that she discovered her sister Aghavni had also survived the Armenian Genocide, the only other member of the family to do so.

The Berlin-based visual artist Silvina Der-Meguerditchian is Aghavni Tenguerian's granddaughter. Silvina grew up with stories of the genocide. She carefully preserves a suitcase full of all kinds of memorabilia connected with relatives who died in those years or survived the genocide. Melkon's tiepin was also in the suitcase. For years Silvina looked for a fitting way to fill the void left by the genocide. She found inspiration in *Houshamadyan*, an online community project 'to reconstruct Ottoman Armenian town and village life'. The aim of the project is to digitally restore the rich, pre-genocide Armenian history that was wiped out during the war. *Houshamadyan* collects and publishes on its website photos, maps, articles on gastronomy, crafts, festivals, religious customs, dialects, songs, and so on produced by the Armenian community in the Ottoman Empire before 1915. The emphasis is on life.

A highlight in Silvina's work is *The Texture of Identity*, a series of 'carpets' in which lost Armenian stories—effectively the Armenian identity—are literally woven together again. Silvina's carpets speak to both collective and personal memory. They deal with loss and nostalgic longing, but also restoration and repair. Silvina's own family story is incorporated, but the *Texture of Identity* symbolises the story of every Armenian family.

Portrait of Shenorhig Tenguerian

Marsovan (Merzifon, Turkey), c. 1919. Armenian and possibly Turkish women and children collect wool from which to weave cloths and clothes for the orphans. The women whose faces are covered may be Armenian converts to Islam. The large striped shawls worn by some of the women are typical of the area around Marsovan (Merzifon).

Shenorhig Tenguerian

Armenian women and children in an orphanage in Ghazir, Lebanon, 1920

Nazan Maksudyan

Nazan MAKSUDYAN

Gendered Violence against Children during the Armenian Genocide

Throughout the First World War, the Committee of Union and Progress (CUP), the ruling political party that monopolised power in 1913, developed a genocidal policy that was to create a homogeneous Muslim population in Anatolia. This biopolitical endeavour, which targeted Armenians as well as other non-Muslim groups, such as Assyrians, was conducted through sexual violence, abduction, adoption, forced marriage, and conversion in an effort to modify the demographic composition of the empire's multi-ethnic and multi-religious population. The main aim was to decimate the male members of the community, thus preventing the Armenian people from procreating and ensuring their demographic future in Anatolia. Armenian religious and civil leadership, together with adult men, were murdered outright at the beginning of the genocide (April–August 1915). Armenian women, girls, and young children were the next major group to be targeted by the Unionist government. After a very short notice of weeks or even hours, all Armenians had to leave their homes and possessions in Anatolia and march to the Syrian desert to be 'relocated'. This was a death march, involving an unending series of dislocations and deportations, exposure, exhaustion, starvation, disease, and epidemics. The remnants of the death marches that managed to reach the Syrian desert were put into concentration camps with no provision of food, water, or medication.

As the concept genocide refers to the extermination of a religious, ethnic, or other group in its entirety, scholars have often treated the 'victims' as a monolithic category. With the progress of research on the Armenian genocide, there is now a more nuanced analysis of violence targeting different groups of victims within the same category of Armenians which has put greater emphasis on the gendered dimension. The literature on the gender-specific aspects of the Armenian genocide has been enriched over the past two decades. New works have examined sexual violence against 'gendered bodies'—in other words, young girls and women—which took the form of rape, kidnapping, abduction, sex slavery, and forced marriages. This enforced assimilation through sexual violence was an outcome of the conviction that ethnic reproduction occurred through the father, not the mother. These historians emphasise that the sexually violent acts were a structural component and a natural extension of the genocidal policies of the Committee of Union and Progress.

Recently, genocide studies have also paid closer attention to the genocidal fate of Armenian children. Valuable research on the oral history of the Armenian genocide is one of the earlier examples in which children (and women) are treated as separate groups of victims who were affected

Talaat Pasha, the Minister of the Interior and one of those chiefly responsible for the genocidal violence that took place in the Ottoman Empire during the First World War

Map illustrating the extent of the Armenian Genocide

differently during the genocide. Research on violence against children has specifically focused on 'ferocious and sadistic methods' with which thousands of Armenian children were murdered. From a gendered perspective on childhood, boys above a certain age—mostly twelve, but sometimes up to fifteen—were usually murdered along with the adult men. This practice stemmed from the definition and limits of childhood. A fifteen-year-old was considered an adult and not a child, and therefore hard to 'recycle'. Mothers often dressed their older boys as a girl to save them. Many survivors' stories stress that this form of disguise was a typical survival strategy for boys, as long as they were not discovered by the guards during the marches. If older boys wanted to stay alive, conversion to Islam offered another opportunity. Fifteen-year-old Aram Haigaz's mother, for instance, knew that her son was in real danger. She convinced him that conversion was the only option for staying alive. By the same token, memoirs reveal that mothers also tried to make their daughters unattractive by blackening their faces or cutting their hair and kept them in the midst of a group to avoid rape and abduction.

Forced deportation to the desert was harder for younger children to endure, whether boys or girls. Many of them lost their lives during the marches due to starvation and disease. However, several orders issued by the CUP made it obvious that younger boys had better chances 'to be saved' by the perpetrators, because they were considered 'children' and not 'Armenian males'. Based on centuries of experience, children could be easily converted to Islam and Turkified, so that they might serve as loyal servants to their masters. Adults were not thought to have the same promise. In July 1915, Ministry of Interior authorised the provinces to collect and distribute Armenian orphans to Muslim families for the purposes of 'care and education'. Later, in April 1916, they specified the 'age limit' as 'up to twelve years old'. Thus, children up to twelve would be handed over to state orphanages, boarding schools, or Muslim households for their upbringing and assimilation (*terbiye ve temsil*)—in other words, in order to Islamicise and Turkify them. The rest of the order makes it apparent that girls older than twelve were either adopted or 'married off', but there is no mention of older boys, suggesting that they were not considered 'victims' to be saved, but rather 'threats' to be eliminated. The genocidal policy of the CUP was to decimate the male members of the community, to prevent them from procreating and thus ensuring that the Armenians did not have a demographic future in Anatolia. In other words, this was a gendered vision of reproduction, privileging the male body and suggesting that lineage was created through the father.

Some Armenian children (young boys and girls) could escape death, as the Ottoman society needed them as labourers, slaves, or concubines. Since population was the salient measure of national power and prestige in the first half of the twentieth century, declining population figures in war years, coupled with nationalist population politics, turned children into a valuable commodity to be possessed. Thousands of Armenian boys and girls were taken into state orphanages (*Darüleytam*), where they were usually used as labour force in workshops. The use of labour was essentially gendered. Boys were trained in shoemaking, carpentry, blacksmithing, turnery (*tornacılık*), bricklaying, and tiling; they were also sent out to the imperial shipyards (*Tersane-i Amire*), the state printing house (*Matbaa-i Amire*), to tanneries (*tabakhane*), and to the 'Chemins de fer Orientaux' (Şark Şimendiferleri Şirketi). State orphanages for girls, which were much less numerous, had workshops for sewing, needlework, and other handicrafts. The girls mostly helped to meet the daily needs of orphanages in cooking and washing. They were introduced to the basics of childcare and home economics. The Ministry of the Interior also transferred hundreds of orphaned children from Anatolia to

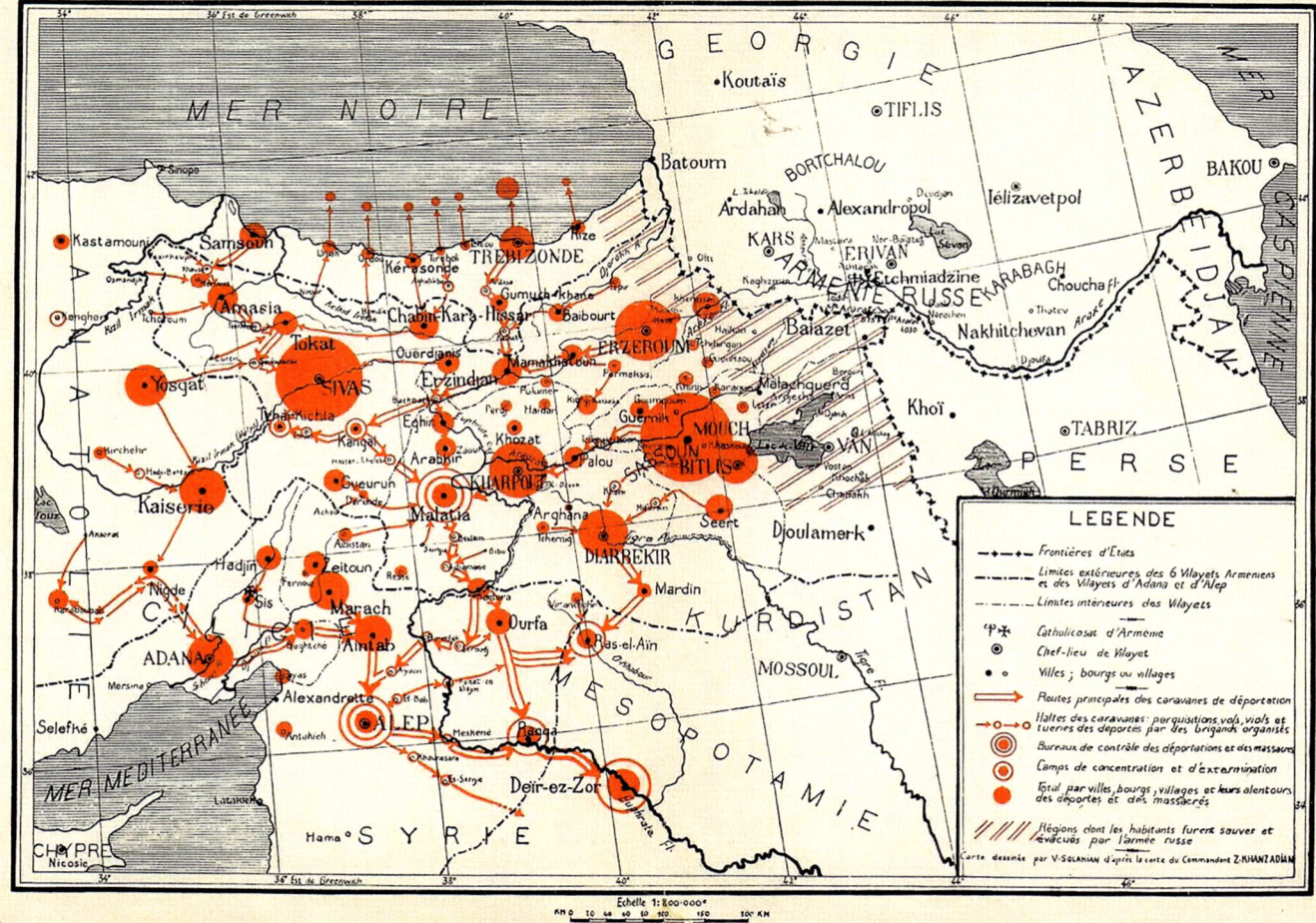

Istanbul through the Society for the Employment of Muslim Women (Kadınları Çalıştırma Cemiyet-i İslâmiyesi). Making use of gendered bodies and labour, the Society distributed (converted) Armenian girls to Muslim households selected by the Ministry, and boys were given away to factories, workshops, ranches, and small businesses in both Istanbul and Anatolia. In these institutions, children were converted to Islam and given Turkish names; the boys were circumcised and raised as Muslim Turks. The main policy of the CUP was to Islamicise and Turkify the children, by conversion, name changes, and by forbidding them to speak Armenian.

The Antoura orphanage of Djemal Pasha, one of the most prominent CUP leaders, who was the governor of the province of Syria at the time, was infamous for its policy of Turkifying Armenian orphans by changing their names to Turkish ones, and by enforcing the exclusive use of Turkish.

Orphans were tormented not only by hunger, but also by unprecedented diseases, ruthless beatings—including a daily bastinado (foot caning) ceremony—and other humiliations. One of the orphans in this institution later wrote that the children were very weak and knew they were fighting 'an unequal battle', but were still 'determined to resist' by clinging to 'their identities, which were all they had left'.

Armenian girls and young women were usually allowed to live if they obeyed their masters and converted to Islam. Girls were sold, bought, forcefully abducted, or stolen by Turkish, Kurdish, and Arab households. There is even evidence that Armenian girls and women were put to auction. In addition to the private acts of seizing, adopting, or selling children, the CUP government gave orders that 'young women and girls be married off to Muslims, so that they will be raised according to Islamic principles'.

Armenian women and children in an orphanage in Ghazir, Lebanon, 1920

The Ministry of Interior also stressed that the state encouraged state officials to 'adopt' Armenian girls into their households. Hundreds of Armenian girls were this way 'adopted' by administrative and military officials. At the end of the First World War, Armenian relief committees and other European and American aid workers estimated that there were at least sixty thousand Armenian boys and girls in Muslim households and state orphanages. Although it is impossible to obtain exact figures, both archival and narrative sources point to a marked difference in the number of girls.

The memoirs of Mabel Evelyn Elliott, a medical doctor who worked at the Scutari Rescue Home (Istanbul)—a shelter for girls escaping Muslim households—are very valuable, as she recounts many of the interviews she had there with the girls. One girl told her story 'in a matter-of-fact voice', as if she 'had lost her sensitiveness'. Her manners were 'bold, almost callous'. She was only twelve years old when the Kurds abducted her. She had been valued because of her youth: they had held her for a higher price while the other girls were being sold. She escaped, and for a year lived a 'phantasmagoria of adventure'. She was captured, escaped again, was wounded, beaten, and hunted. She also got a knife and used it to kill. Driven by starvation, on several occasions she sought out Muslim households and was taken in, but escaped the moment she realised she was going to be sold as a slave: once she wrenched bars from windows, and another time she jumped off the wall.

When incorporated into Muslim households—in other words, converted to Islam, married to and impregnated by Muslim men, and subjected to patriarchal power within the family—young women and girls were considered less threatening and more formable by the CUP leaders. From the perspective of nationalist population politics, the government exerted control over Armenian women's bodies, sexuality, marital behaviour, and reproduction. Forced marital conversions were part of the genocidal violence and instrumental in increasing the Muslim population. Moreover, the patriarchal culture of honour in Ottoman communities also made women more vulnerable to sexual violence in another way. Since the chastity of women was assumed to be inherently connected to the nation's honour and identity, and thus given great symbolic value, Turkish perpetrators' sexual violence targeting Armenian women and girls must be seen as part of the genocidal violence.

Armenian boys below a certain age and girls had a greater chance of survival thanks to their importance as a demographic resource. Unlike Nazi racial policies during the Holocaust, the CUP's systematic and genocidal policy towards Armenian children pointed to more of a *tabula rasa* understanding of human resources. These children born of Christian Armenian parents could still be forcefully assimilated into the Turkish/Muslim nation and raised as Muslim Turks. There is also the need to underline that neither adoption nor conversion and assimilation were Unionist discoveries. The Ottoman dynasty and society

Armenian women and children in an orphanage in Ghazir, Lebanon, 1920

had older traditions, such as the *devshirme* practice (to recruit young boys in the bureaucracy and the army) and concubinage (to procreate), both inalienable to Ottoman slavery. The long-lived *besleme* tradition, through which better-off families 'adopted' the daughters of poorer families to use them as maidservants and abuse them as concubines, was also an ancestor of CUP the policy.

Taken together, the words genocide and children inevitably conjure up tragic images. As in Armin T. Wegner's photographs of Armenian children in 1915–16, we envision starving, crying, and dying children, their emaciated bodies lying on the barren ground. These are visions of a cruel historical reality and capture what happened to many children during the genocide. The existing historiography of the Armenian genocide largely focuses on child victims, who were bought, sold, kidnapped, or rescued. In contrast, there is need to consider another image, that of surviving Armenian children. These youngest witnesses and survivors of the genocide can also be portrayed as 'agents' with a say in their own fates. In fact, self-representation in survivors' narratives is not only one of victimisation, but also of resilience. Survival narratives depict an Armenian child-hero who is not only rebellious, but also superior to an inhumane and coercive society of cruel, malevolent, and insensitive adults.

Armenian children survived under paradoxical circumstances: they were targets (and hence victims) of direct violence, sexual exploitation, and the erasure of identity, but they were also agents who tried to fight back through escape, pretence, and resistance. In the context of the genocide, children's agency was not a limitless 'capacity' or one that could bring progressive change. Agency mostly constituted the capacity to endure and suffer. The agency of Armenian survivors was also relative to several social structures, especially age, gender, and solidarity. Older children took responsibility for younger ones, such that children's agency was usually expressed and realised in solidarity with other children. Gendered aspects of genocidal violence against boys and girls also affected their agency and survival strategies. Survival stories of child victims who suffered through innumerable acts of violence, loss, and trauma also portray proud and self-confident survivors who came 'through hell alive'. The narratives bring to light several aspects of genocidal violence, but also the genocide survivor's agency.

Ihsan TURJMAN

1893–1917

The First World War violently disrupted the familiar patterns within Ottoman society. Hundreds of thousands of men were marched away from their home environments and sent to the front. Many never returned. Women had to take on new roles, and children were deployed in the war economy, just to survive. In 1917 and 1918, some of the orphaned boys were even sent to Germany to work in mines or on farms.

The Ottoman world was not only a stage for the violence of war or repression against minority groups, but also for diseases, epidemics, and famines. As if that were not enough, in 1915 what would later become Lebanon, Palestine, and large parts of Syria was struck by a devastating plague of locusts. In Lebanon, that disaster resulted in a famine which lasted until the end of the war and cost more than a hundred thousand lives. In late March 1915, Ihsan Turjman was working as a clerk in the Jerusalem administration when he noted in his diary:

> 'Heavy rain fell over Jerusalem today, which we needed badly. Locusts are attacking all over the country. The locust invasion started seven days ago and covered the sky. Today it took the locust clouds two hours to pass over the city. God protect us from the three plagues: war, locusts, and disease, for they are spreading through the country. Pity the poor.'

Ihsan's diary gives us fascinating evidence of everyday life behind the Ottoman lines. His observations are not purely anecdotal but include political reflections on the impact of the war as well. He also thought about what the future would bring. On 28 March 1915, for example, he wrote:

> 'We more or less agreed that the days of the state are numbered and that its dismemberment is imminent. But what will be the fate of Palestine? We all saw two possibilities: independence or annexation to Egypt. The last possibility is more likely since only the English are likely to possess this country, and England is unlikely to give full sovereignty to Palestine but is more liable to annex it to Egypt and create a single dominion ruled by the Khedive of Egypt. Egypt is our neighbour, and since both countries contain a majority of Muslims, it makes sense to annex it and crown the viceroy of Egypt as king of Palestine and Hejaz.'

Ihsan would never know what the future held for Palestine. In 1917, he was called up for military service and was killed in Jerusalem in December that year, just before the entry of British troops.

Portrait of Ihsan Turjman

It seems to be raining locusts. The locust plague began in March 1915 in the Syria, Lebanon, and Palestine region and was not brought under control until October. The 1915 summer and autumn harvests (fruits and vegetables) were almost completely destroyed.

Even flamethrowers were used to get rid of the pests.

Ihsan TURJMAN

The infamous Sykes-Picot Agreement: the division of the Ottoman Empire into French and British spheres of influence. The map was signed at the beginning of May 1916 (lower right corner) by the architects of the agreement, Mark Sykes and François Georges-Picot.

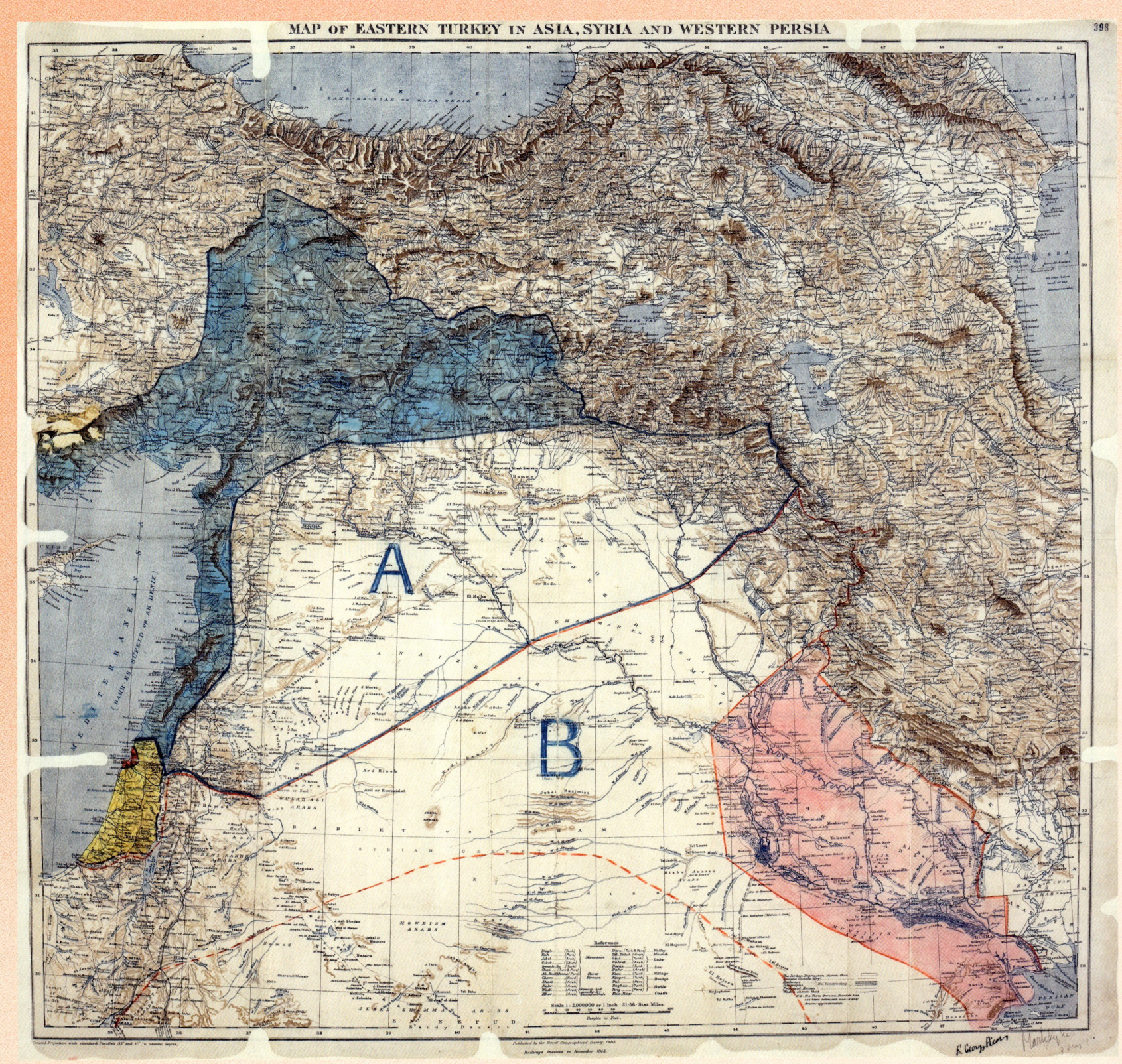

Alp YENEN

Between Imperialism and Revolution: Geopolitics of the Great War in the Middle East

There are two classic ways of studying the history of wars. On the one hand, historians can look at wars as international events, as conflicts between states. Such a perspective tries to explain why and how states engage in collisions and coalitions with other states on the battlefield and at diplomatic conferences in order to win the war. On the other hand, historians can study a single nation, because internal affairs could be determining state behaviour in wars. Such histories try to explain how wars affect state-society relations and how the outcome of wars is dictated by national policies, economic resources, and social forces at a national level. Beyond these classic approaches, most contemporary historians have come to appreciate that both international and national dimensions of war need to be combined, because states also interact with the societies of other states. This was ever more the case with the emergence of the idea of 'total war' in the First World War. In total wars, the line between the military and civil society as well as between combatants and non-combatants disappears. States not only mobilise their own societies for the war effort and antagonise foreign societies as enemies that must be destroyed, but also look for potential collaborators among foreign populations within enemy states and fear subversion and treason in their own societies. This crisscrossing of states and societies across borders is a crucial aspect of studying the geopolitics of the First World War at a global scale.

Imperialism and revolution were two strategies of geopolitics through which states and societies interacted with one another in the Middle Eastern theatre of the First World War. Ideas of imperialism and revolution were meant to control and co-opt foreign populations against their states to bring an end to the war. Especially in the Balkans, where the First World War started, there was a century-old history of entanglement between imperialism and revolution since the Greek War of Independence (1821–1829). While European monarchies were wary of revolutionary movements against themselves, they had supported the Greek revolutionaries in their struggle for liberation from the Ottoman Empire. Make no mistake, European great powers were not conspiring for the collapse of the Ottoman Empire. The so-called 'Eastern Question', a contemporary euphemism in diplomacy for the geopolitical game of controlling the decline of the Ottoman Empire without disturbing the balance of power in the Concert of Europe, would actually help the Ottoman sultans to survive threats of military and economic collapse throughout the nineteenth century. Nevertheless, the Ottoman Empire as well as the Khedivate of Egypt and Qajar Empire of Persia became entangled in semi-colonial contractions under the so-called capitulations that allowed privileges for European policies and businesses. Meanwhile, the frontier regions of the wider Middle East in North Africa, the Caucasus, and Central and South Asia could not escape the fate of colonisation by French, Russian, and British empires throughout the nineteenth century. The rise of Germany under Prussian rule as a new European great power further aggravated geopolitical struggles. The two Berlin Congresses (1878 and 1884–5) not only created the conditions for future conflict at the frontiers of empires in the Balkans and Caucasus, where imperial ambitions and nationalist-revolutionary activism collided with one other after the end of the Russo-Turkish War of 1877–8, but also shaped a new imperialism and colonialism in the so-called 'Scramble for Africa'. It was at the Berlin Congress of 1878,

In the second half of the nineteenth century, the Ottoman Empire lost several territories (coloured yellow on the map): Bosnia, Serbia, Montenegro, Romania, Bulgaria, Eastern Rumelia, and Thessaly.

In 1913, the Young Turks staged a violent coup that brought them to power in the Ottoman Empire.

where the Ottoman province of Bosnia-Herzegovina was put under the administration of the Austro-Hungarian Empire, that the stage would be set for the triggering of the First World War in the summer of 1914.

At the turn of the century, imperialism and revolution continued to shape the contours of conflicts. Due to imperial misgovernance, the Ottoman Empire was challenged by rebellions in various frontiers, including Western Armenia, Macedonia, Yemen, and Albania. The emergence of new revolutionary committees that operated both as political parties and insurgent bands, as well as new forms of revolutionary action nourished by the influx of military surplus weapons and easy access to explosives, worsened state-society relations and intensified intercommunal violence. Imperial competition in the Middle East increased when Germany's advances into the Middle East to carve 'a place in the sun' for Kaiser Wilhelm II's grand schemes pushed the British and Russian empires towards rapprochement to settle their differences in the so-called 'Great Game'. Against the backdrop of this imperial settlement between Britain and Russia, constitutional revolutions took place in the Qajar and Ottoman empires that founded parliaments and introduced elections. The revolution in the Ottoman Empire was organised by the so-called 'Young Turks', a revolutionary committee of Muslim military officers, petty bureaucrats, and exiled intellectuals. They were concerned about the fate of the Ottoman Empire's Balkan provinces and inspired by the methods of Macedonian and Armenian revolutionaries. Reactions of the European great powers to the constitutional revolutions in Turkey and Iran were rather negative. British officials were concerned that it would inspire anticolonialism in Egypt and India. The Russian Empire intervened militarily in the civil war after the Persian constitutional revolution on behalf of monarchist and counterrevolutionary forces. Seizing the opportunity of the constitutional revolution, the Austro-Hungarian Empire unilaterally annexed Bosnia-Herzegovina in 1908, and Italy occupied Ottoman provinces in Libya in 1911. While Austrian goods were boycotted as a means of non-violent protest, Young Turk officers volunteered for the defence of Libya, where they conducted an unconventional war along with Arab nationalists, Bedouin tribes, and religious orders. The Turkish-Italian War was interrupted by the First Balkan War in 1912, when a coalition of ex-Ottoman states declared war on the Ottoman Empire and took away most of its European territories. The Young Turks, who had been ousted by the opposition, took over the government through a coup d'état in 1913 and tried to reconquer some of the lost territories in the Second Balkan War. The Balkan Wars were the prelude to the First World War as a total war, in that revolutionary and military forces fought side by side on behalf of state interests, and enemy civil populations were purged and persecuted in accordance with national demographic imperatives. After the loss of the European provinces, the Ottoman Empire became more Muslim than ever before. Young Turk leadership became irreversibly resentful, as most of them had lost their homelands in Ottoman Macedonia. At the nexus of international and national politics, Young Turk leaders became convinced that international law was working against the interests of Muslim peoples. Consequently, the loyalty of Christian populations in the Ottoman Empire became questionable in their eyes. After establishing what amounted to a single-party dictatorship, Young Turk leaders believed that a Third Balkan War, possibly against Greece, would escalate in 1914, and hoped to use it to recover past losses and save the integrity of the Ottoman Empire. However, the next Balkan War did not start between Turkey and Greece, but rather between Austria-Hungary and Serbia after the assassination of Archduke Franz Ferdinand by 'Young Bosnian' revolutionaries on 28 June 1914. The chain reaction

Autochrome of Turkish refugees from Edirne. During the Balkan Wars (1912–1913) the Ottoman Empire lost almost all its territories on the European mainland. Muslims living in those areas were massacred or forced to flee in great numbers because of the war.

of imperial alliances turned the diplomatic crisis of July 1914 into a European war, and after the entrance of the Ottomans into a global war that was fought on three continents.

Despite the will to reverse the ill-fated situation of the Ottoman Empire, the Young Turk government knew that their military was in a desolate state after the defeats against the Balkan states. Moreover, after Turkey's former allies France and England formed an entente together with the Turkey's archenemy Russia, their diplomacy was isolated. Ottoman proposals to join the Entente were rejected, pushing the Young Turks towards an alliance with the Central Powers of Germany and Austria-Hungary (later joined by Bulgaria). The Ottoman alliance was kept secret from the public to allow the Ottoman military to mobilise under the pretext of defensive neutrality. After the British navy seized two vessels, which had been purchased by the Ottoman navy through a public funding campaign, the Young Turk government and the public were enraged. Germany offered the Ottoman navy two of its own warships, the *Goeben* and the *Breslau*, which were being pursued by British vessels in the Mediterranean and seeking a safe haven in Ottoman waters. The formal entry of the Ottoman Empire into the war, which Young Turk leadership wanted to postpone in the face of German pressure, took place on 28 October 1914, when the two ships mentioned above opened fire on the Russian fleet in the Black Sea. The Ottoman contribution to the war effort of the Central Powers was meant to divert the attention of the Entente Powers from the war theatres of Central and Eastern Europe towards North Africa, Middle East, Caucasus, and Central Asia. All Entente states possessed ex-Ottoman territories and other Muslim countries as colonial possessions: Algeria and Tunisia had been under French rule since 1830 and 1881, respectively; in addition, France controlled Morocco since 1912; Britain, the greatest Muslim empire of its time thanks to India, had occupied Egypt, which was nominally under Ottoman suzerainty, in 1882 and unilaterally declared it a protectorate in 1914; Russia had annexed three Ottoman provinces at the Anatolian-Caucasian frontier back in 1878, in addition to its Muslim populations in Crimea, Caucasus, and Central Asia; Italy entered war in 1916 and possessed ex-Ottoman provinces in Libya and the Dodecanese Islands since 1912. Besides diverting resources from the European theatre of war, the direct strategy of the Ottoman military—based on ideas of imperial irredentism—also aimed at reconquering some of its lost territories, for example, during the military campaigns against Egypt and Caucasus in the winter of 1915.

This Ottoman imperial strategy had also a revolutionary dimension. On 11 November 1914, the Ottoman government's chief of religious affairs declared an Islamic holy war on behalf of the Sultan-Caliph, who was considered the spiritual sovereign of all Muslims in the world. The Ottoman jihad campaign was organised by Ottoman military intelligence officers and German propagandists to revolutionise the Muslim subjects of the Entente empires in a global anticolonial rebellion. Ottoman agents and special forces were sent to North Africa, Caucasus, Central Asia, and South Asia to incite local rebellions. Muslim political and religious leaders from colonial lands were invited to the Ottoman capital to campaign for the holy war. Attempts were made to convince Muslim rulers in Persia and Afghanistan to join the war on the side of the Central Powers. Propaganda publications were translated into multiple local languages and dispatched to far corners of the Muslim world. Muslim prisoners of war were recruited to serve in the Ottoman army. Most of these ambitious efforts were, however, to no avail. No such Muslim uprising took place, except for the mostly unrelated anti-conscription revolt of Turkic tribes against Russian authorities in Central Asia in 1916. Moreover, Muslim soldiers from Africa, Central Asia, and India fought in Entente armies on all fronts.

The 'Intikam' or 'Revenge' map, published by the Society of Muslim Refugees from Rumelia, shows the part of the Ottoman Empire (coloured in black) that was lost during the Balkan Wars and from which these refugees fled.

Nevertheless, the Ottoman jihad was more effective on the home front, as it helped mass military mobilisation by giving it a global social justice cause. The Ottoman calls for jihad against European 'Crusaders' and local 'infidels' maintained solidarity among Sunnis and Shi'ites as well as among Turks, Arabs, and Kurds of the Ottoman Empire.

The most tragic outcome of the imperial and revolutionary strategies of the Ottoman war effort was the Armenian Genocide of 1915. Armenians resided across the Turkish, Russian, and Persian imperial frontiers. Although the Young Turks had tried to build an alliance with Armenian revolutionaries against the Russian Empire, this was not realised. After the Ottoman defeat in the Caucasus campaign of 1915, the Armenian population was blamed for collaboration with the enemy and suspected of preparing for a great insurgency. The foundation of Armenian volunteer battalions in the Russian army further enhanced such public paranoias. After a political purge of the Armenian political elite in Istanbul, most of the Armenian population of Anatolia was displaced from their homes to settle in Syria. The deportation of Armenians, which soon included the Assyrians as well, was accompanied by death marches, paramilitary massacres, abduction of women and children, and confiscation of property that reached a genocidal extent. While the Young Turks' regime had a clear nationalist agenda in cleansing Anatolia of non-Muslim elements as a new homeland for Ottoman Muslims, there were also international and imperial security concerns based on the contingencies of the war that opened the path for catastrophe.

Meanwhile, the Entente Powers had in fact their own imperial schemes and revolutionary plots for the destruction of the Ottoman Empire and division of its spoils. The Sykes-Picot Agreement of May 1916 between Britain and France, as well as the addendum treaties with Russia and Italy, foresaw territorial expansions and the extension of colonial spheres of influence. The Ottoman Middle East reaching into the Turkish-Arab and Arab-Kurdish borderlands of Anatolia was divided between Britain and France. Istanbul, the Straits, and Western Armenia were promised to Russia. Italy laid claim to the Mediterranean coast of Anatolia. In the Middle East, imperial plans were complicated by British intelligence activities to stir up Arab nationalism against the Ottoman Empire. Although the Young Turks had been investing in the Arab provinces to preserve the empire as a Muslim state, relations between Arab and Turkish nationalists were tense and characterised by mutual distrust. Chauvinistic and despotic measures taken by Turkish wartime governors in the Arab provinces, especially against Arab nationalists suspected of espionage, further aggravated the situation. The Ottoman guardian of Mecca, Sharif Hussein, made a secret deal with the British to start an Arab revolt in return for the promise of an independent Arabia reaching from the Hejaz to the Levant. Promises made to the Arabs conflicted with French plans for Syria, and soon also contradicted the Balfour declaration to Zionists to create a 'Jewish homeland' in Palestine. The Arab Revolt of 1916 did not receive much popular support among Arabs, who largely remained loyal to the Ottomans, but thanks to the British military intelligence, including men like T. E. Lawrence (of Arabia), it changed the course of the war in its Middle Eastern theatre by occupying Ottoman military resources.

While the offensive campaigns of the Ottomans had failed terribly in Caucasus and Egypt, the Ottoman army proved to be more effective defending the Dardanelles and Mesopotamia. These two fronts were part of the British strategy to encircle the Ottoman heartlands and connect with the Russian military in the Black Sea and Eastern Anatolia. This strategy failed, as Ottoman defence was effective. Meanwhile, a revolutionary plot was conceived in Istanbul when Alexander Helphand (Parvus), a famous revolutionary of his time, proposed a plan to the German Ambassador to support the Bolsheviks in their efforts to stir up a revolution in the Russia Empire. The Russian Revolution of 1917 had immediate consequences for the Ottoman war effort, as it relieved pressure on the Eastern front. Moreover, Bolshevik leadership publicised the secret treaties for the partition of the Ottoman Empire by the Entente Powers. These treaties very much confirmed the embittered worldview of the Young Turks and disappointed the leaders of the Arab Revolt, who had relied on British promises. The retreat of the Russian military from Eastern Anatolia and the Caucasus created an opportunity for the Ottoman-German alliance to launch a new Caucasus campaign. Instead of imperial expansion—apart from the three previously lost provinces—the Young Turks wanted to create a *cordon sanitaire* of friendly regimes in Georgia, Armenia, Azerbaijan, and beyond in Dagestan and Crimea.

Despite the Ottoman conquest of Baku with the help of Azerbaijani troops in September 1918, the war was lost on the Syrian and Mesopotamian fronts. The surrender of Bulgaria rendered the Ottoman capital defenceless on the Balkan front. The Ottoman Empire signed an armistice on 30 October 1918. However, contrary to expectations, achieving peace in the Middle East would prove to be difficult. Despite international pressure, the Young Turks could not be properly prosecuted for the war crimes against Armenians and would even remain influential after the war. Although the Ottoman military was demobilised, a war of independence soon succeeded in uprooting plans for the partition of Turkey. Regardless of all the international support, Greece was unable extend it territories into Anatolia, nor could an independent Armenia survive. Even though the Arabs were considered liberated from the 'Turkish yoke', revolts and revolutions challenged colonial settlements in Egypt, Palestine, Syria, and Iraq. Instead of the expected rise of ethnic-nationalism, collaboration between Turks, Arabs, and Kurds continued against the peace settlement. While the Ottoman jihad of 1914 had failed to animate pan-Islamic solidarity in the Muslim world, a global movement of Muslim internationalism from Morocco to India emerged after 1919 in opposition to the partition of the Ottoman Empire. Muslim countries that had not joined the Ottoman war effort, such as Persia and Afghanistan, built up new alliances against European great powers. Although Russia was ousted from the European Concert after the take-over of the Bolsheviks, Soviet Russia became a force to be reckoned with in the peace settlement in the Middle East. The Arab leaders who had led the Arab Revolt of 1916 would become kings under colonial administrations. Among all the defeated countries, ironically, Turkey would emerge with regained sovereignty and a new revolutionary ethos. In many ways, the armistice period would turn into a prolongation of the war but reverse the geopolitics of imperialism and revolution.

FAISAL

1882–1933

In the Western world, the Arab Revolt (1916–1918) against the Ottoman-Turkish regime is often still seen as having been successfully engineered by T. E. Lawrence—also known as Lawrence of Arabia. Naturally, that perception is in part connected with David Lean's 1962 blockbuster film. In reality, however, many others contributed to the revolt. One of the figureheads was Prince Faisal, the third of four sons of Sharif Hussein, of the Hejaz region. Faisal was educated in Constantinople and had embraced the liberal, modern ideals of the constitutional revolution (1908) in the Ottoman Empire.

In 1915, the British initiated discussions with Sharif Hussein about a potential Arab uprising against the Ottomans in return for a post-war independent Arab state. Faisal undertook a mission to create as much support as possible for an Arab nationalist revolt. Hussein and the British reached an agreement (McMahon-Hussein Correspondence) and in June 1916 the Arab Revolt began.

Faisal commanded the Arab 'Northern Army'. His troops were made up of former Ottoman soldiers sympathetic to the Arab cause and unattached Bedouin desert tribes. The military campaign first ran along the coast of present-day Saudi Arabia and soon gained British support. Faisal later advanced further towards Syria. In 1917 and 1918, the period of the attacks on the Hejaz Railway, he developed a close friendship with T. E. Lawrence. In early October 1918, Faisal captured Damascus with the help of Allied troops. A few days later, he proclaimed the Arab Kingdom of Syria, which would roughly encompass (present-day) Israel and Palestine, Syria, Lebanon and Jordan.

In the spring of 1919, Faisal led an Arab delegation to the Paris Peace Conference to secure the new state in accordance with the promises made by Britain in 1915. When it appeared that the British were now less enthusiastic, and the French claimed 'their' Lebanon and Syria (in accordance with the Sykes-Picot Agreement), a disenchanted Faisal returned to Damascus to organise the founding of an independent 'Greater Syria' himself. He established an Arab national government, held democratic elections, and had a modern, liberal constitution drafted. The power of the king was curtailed, Islam was abolished as the state religion, and Muslims and non-Muslims were given the same rights.

In March 1920, Syrian independence was declared. The French refused to recognise it, and that summer they invaded the territory and expelled Faisal from it. Syria became a French mandate, a euphemism for a colony. The French regarded Syrians as 'incapable of self-government', an imperialist perspective that is also highlighted in the closing scenes of Lean's *Lawrence of Arabia*. The British reclaimed Faisal and in 1921 installed him as king of Iraq—now a British mandate. The erasure of Syria's short-lived democratic past left deep wounds in Syrian society.

T. E. Lawrence and Prince Faisal (centre), en route to the Paris Peace Conference in 1919

93   **Portrait of Faisal I, King of Iraq,** *c.* **1930**   Faisal

Nicholas J. SAUNDERS

The Pillars of Belief: T. E. Lawrence and the Archaeology of the Arab Revolt, 1916–2014

Thomas E. Lawrence was and remains an enigmatic and controversial figure in the twentieth century history of the Middle East, his legacy shaped mainly by the enduring influence of his guerrilla activities in the Arab Revolt of 1916–18 as recorded in his 1926 *Seven Pillars of Wisdom*. Although controversy still swirls around Lawrence and his book, a unique opportunity to assess part of his legacy—his reliability as a military historian chronicling Arab and British attacks on the Ottoman Hejaz Railway—came with the creation of the University of Bristol's Great Arab Revolt Project (GARP), which ran from 2005 until 2014. Testing Lawrence's veracity was not the aim of the archaeological and anthropological investigations, but the entanglement of history with myth, literature, cinema, and more recent Middle Eastern military and political events meant that archaeology offered a new and clear line of investigation.

Much of what has been written about Lawrence has focused on his complex personality, his disillusionment and sense of betrayal with the politics of post-war events, his retreat from public life after 1922, and his 1935 death in a motorcycle accident in southern England. Much criticism has been aimed at his claiming credit for the Arab Revolt achievements of others (British comrades and Bedouin), despite his own admission that his reputation was founded upon fraud, and how *Seven Pillars* was not a history of the Arab Revolt but purely about what had happened to himself. Perhaps one of the most piercing comments about the book was made in 1975 by Albert Hourani, who regarded it as 'an attempt to write an epic work about activities that themselves had been moulded by a person who intended to write about them.'

During our research, we encountered varying attitudes toward Lawrence: some Arabs regarded him with contempt as little more than a self-aggrandising imperialist agent for the British who betrayed the Arab cause. Others took pride in recalling how their distant relations had ridden with Lawrence against the Turk, and surprisingly to us, there were those who recalled with pride 'riding' with Peter O'Toole in David Lean's 1962 Hollywood epic *Lawrence of Arabia*. Our project was an avowedly interdisciplinary endeavour, situated at the crossroads of different kinds of memory—Arab, Ottoman Turkish, Western technological/ imperial, military, cultural—and existing also in oral tradition and literary forms. And in this sense, it is worth remembering that Lawrence himself admitted that *Seven Pillars of Wisdom* was a memory of a memory—written

T. E. Lawrence in Arab robes, 1918

T. E. Lawrence and Leonard Woolley (right) pose by a Hittite artefact in Carchemish, Syria, 1912.

in 1919 from recall and notes, then apparently lost, then rewritten from memory again and amended between late 1919 and 1922. It is unsurprising that these momentous historical events were remembered and interpreted differently by all concerned.

Regardless of many countervailing flows of historical reality, attitudes, memory, and books which saw him either as a brilliant and perceptive observer and participant or as an almost worthless fraud, Lawrence has for many become heroically emblematic of the Arab Revolt. This image was burnished by David Lean's film in ways which appealed to public sensibilities of Britain and the world up until the 1960s, but which are far more problematic today.

The fog which shrouds the historical Lawrence in myth and controversy has often been a barrier to understanding certain aspects of his true role, despite his being endlessly written about since his death (and still today in a steady stream of new publications). But it is possible to glimpse the reality, albeit imperfectly, in the physical remains of the Arab Revolt which still litter the desert wadis of Jordan and Saudi Arabia. It is all too easy to dismiss Lawrence as a liar and fabricator or exalt him as an all-seeing genius if one has no experience of the landscapes in which he fought between 1916 and 1918.

The Great Arab Revolt Project (GARP)

GARP aimed to investigate archaeologically the hitherto largely uncharted conflict landscapes of the Arab Revolt in southern Jordan. After a year's reconnaissance, there followed nine years of annual fieldwork mainly in the area stretching from Ma'an south to the border with Saudi Arabia—a distance of 113 km. While the original intention had been to investigate the damaged and mostly abandoned Hejaz Railway stations along this route, it soon became evident that there existed previously unrecognised and undocumented conflict landscapes in-between these stations and farther out in the desert.

While proving or disproving Lawrence's account of his actions in this area was not the aim, nevertheless, history and myth sometimes collided in the archaeology, and our investigations provided surprising verifiable historical information and insight unavailable to all who had written about Lawrence since 1918, and especially since his death. In other words, after 100 years, it was possible to say something fresh, to present dramatic new physical evidence, and to add insightful perspectives by breathing new life and meaning into photographic and documentary archive records. Several examples illustrate how Lawrence's ideas and actions are supported by archaeological evidence.

In a much-quoted passage from *Seven Pillars*, Lawrence writes about spending the night in the desert with a Rolls Royce Armoured Car group the night before a raid on the Hejaz Railway. He recalls how 'We slept there that chilly night, happy with bully-beef and tea and biscuit, with English talk and laughter round the fire, golden with its shower of sparks from the fierce brushwood'. Such intimate views were repeated by his driver S. C. Rolls, who recorded Lawrence and his men sitting around a campfire and drinking the strong rum ration. Despite the fame of Lawrence's passage, nobody knew what this camp was called or where it was. GARP's investigations discovered the answers: the place was Tooth Hill Camp (in fact two camps—THC West and THC East), and through a mix of archival research and field walking the site was rediscovered in 2012, some ninety-four years after it had been abandoned.

Not only this, but the campsite was so well preserved that it was as if Lawrence and his comrades had left only a few days before. Vehicle spark plugs, a mass of empty bullet cartridges, smashed rum jars and gin bottles, and, crucially, dated bully-beef tins were convincing, as was the excavation of several campfires revealing the remains of burnt brushwood. Archaeology had retrieved the preserved material remains of an event written about by Lawrence in *Seven Pillars*, an event which had lasted but a few short hours.

Equally ephemeral was the temporary canvas-hangar landing strip of Disi, one of several 'Advanced Landing Grounds' (ALGs) from where British RAF biplanes flew reconnaissance missions and then bombed the Hejaz Railway and its stations. Lawrence recorded how he had visited in May 1918 in a car full of rations for pilots and support staff who were based at 'Disi mud-flat by [Wadi] Rum, to bomb Ma'an and Mudowwara at ease'. Trying to find a transient landing ground (i.e., simply a convenient mudflat) used for just a few months in the vastness of the desert looked like a hopeless task, and for several years it was. Eventually, with the help of our network of Bedouin contacts and several contemporary black-and-white photos from private collections, we found the site, and confirmed it by excavation and the finding of hearths and .303 cartridges.

Arguably the most famous guerrilla action that Lawrence was involved with, and which became iconic through his description of it and, later, David Lean's film, was the train ambush at Hallat Ammar on 18 September 1917. Lawrence's daring and bravery in reconnoitring the site, spending five hours laying a fifty-pound gelignite charge by the bridge, and then participating in the violence which followed the explosion, derailment, and Bedouin looting were all too real. His *Seven Pillars* account was verified by GARP, which had access to this area (today a no-man's land on the Jordan-Saudi Arabia border), where his description was matched by excavation evidence of the spread of small arms fire across the desert, and the presence of shattered steel railway sleepers.

The spectacular success of the ambush paid several dividends. First, it destroyed two Ottoman locomotives and their wagons, but it also boosted Bedouin respect for Lawrence and showed that any future attack on the nearby Ottoman station at Mudawwara would need a large force if it was to be successful. Hallat Ammar demonstrated the power of guerrilla warfare, in that surprise, speed, weaponry, and knowledge of the local landscape were key elements, although not a guarantee, of success.

It is worth saying that in nine years of walking, surveying, and excavating the desert and interviewing the Bedouin, we came to know this region at least as well as Lawrence. This was because he had spent just short albeit intense periods there, whereas we had the luxury of visiting and revisiting places for nine years without being in mortal danger. This gave us the opportunity to scout for new sites and follow up leads. Some of the sites we discovered did not appear in the archives or *Seven Pillars* because they had no Ottoman soldiers at the time Lawrence passed through or RAF aeroplanes flew over—and so were not worth recording militarily. Blending into the desert landscape, some sites were never seen, except by their Ottoman builders. Other sites left little or no documentary trace because Lawrence was not personally present to write about them; others have only a faint archival mention, but often we were able to locate, identify, and provide an archaeological signature for them. In other words, GARP recorded many Arab Revolt sites that for various reasons were invisible to the Arabs and the British during the Revolt and/or had remained that way since 1918.

Wadi Rum: Ottoman Army campsite showing Ottoman spoons, padlock, star-and-crescent army button, and prehistoric tool

Shattered steel railway sleeper at the site of the 1917 Hallat Ammar ambush

Landscape photograph of the Hejaz Railway, probably somewhere near Al-'Ula (Saudi Arabia), 1916

Lawrence and the 'Bedu Way'

Insights into Lawrence's undoubted affinity with the Bedouin and his ability to 'read' the desert and its military opportunities has often been remarked upon. Importantly, and uniquely, he theorised and codified this blend of traditional Arab raiding and Western technology in his famous *Twenty-Seven Articles* published in 1917. Here, amongst other things, he advocated learning the Bedu principles of war, concentrating forces only for momentary tactical superiority, making maximum use of mobility, and making war on matériel not men. In many ways these ideas have left their material traces on the desert—in the overnight camps of the Arab-British insurgency, and in the scattered small fortifications of the ultimately unsuccessful Ottoman counter-insurgency efforts. The archaeological evidence is the concrete legacy of a theory of something new—motorised guerrilla warfare, for which Lawrence was such a vocal advocate.

Every year GARP spent in the desert it became clearer that Lawrence was in many ways ahead of the curve in military thinking in Arabia, by adopting Bedouin behaviour, tactics, and living with the desert not against it. His unusual views and non-traditional military thinking proved a positive advantage in moving around the desert like a vapour, as he said, unpredictably, and then striking the enemy out of the blue with a hammer blow. His colleague Colonel P. C. Joyce, who by 1918 was Feisal's chief British liaison officer, recalled his experiences of driving through the desert with Lawrence in his Rolls Royce tender 'Blue Mist': 'we tore across sand dunes and ridges under his almost uncanny guidance [a number of the men who accompanied Lawrence in the desert have remarked upon his ability to recall the location of a bush, a rise, or a rock after he had once seen it]...'. Such skills were impressive for a non-Bedouin, but so was Lawrence's ability to comprehend how such knowledge could be combined with and emphasised by Western military technologies.

A prime example of this, as we have seen above, was his championing of the Hejaz Armoured Car Company, with its ability to move rapidly and with deadly effect against the railway and Turkish positions. Lawrence's valuing of these vehicles on his own side extended to his appreciation of their absence by the Ottomans. In an oft-overlooked passage from a 1923 letter Lawrence wrote to Archibald Wavell, that 'If the Turks had put machine guns on three or four of their touring cars, & driven them on weekly patrol over [the desert] they would have put an absolute stop to our ... rebellion ... [Instead] They scraped up cavalry & armoured trains and camel corps & blockhouses against us: because they didn't think hard enough'. Lawrence clearly saw the nature and advantages of such vehicles. And Wavell clearly agreed as his view was that 'For absolute mobility—intangibility, in fact—the Arab raiding forces under Lawrence were unsurpassable'.

GARP's discovery and excavation of the transient overnight raiding campsites gave a modern scientific verification of the size, location, and importance of such sites. The Tooth Hill Camps were the more than 100-year-old footprint of asymmetrical warfare that Lawrence had midwifed into being. And in a typical literary flourish after one such lightning raid, he observed that 'A Rolls in the desert was above rubies'.

Seven Pillars of Wisdom is one of the great war accounts; not just because of its literary merits, its length and detail, or its troubled and convoluted publishing history, and the alternating attitudes of its author—one moment a hero, the next a self-confessed fraud—but because many of the key events of the Arab Revolt at which he was present align his story with the archaeology. As an archaeologist himself, Lawrence may have been bemused by our efforts.

But despite his book's faults and errors, several key points ring true. It captures and transmits a coherent account of events which archaeological investigations showed to be remarkably accurate in many respects. And, intriguingly, Lawrence sometimes sat and camped just a metre or so away from prehistoric artifacts (some of which he saw, others not, and many of which we found). Together with his Arab and British comrades, and indeed his Ottoman antagonists, he created new archaeological layers of the conflict landscape palimpsest.

Lawrence's legacy today is contested, and will likely remain so, but his passion for the cleansing desert, its Bedouin inhabitants, his talent for guerrilla warfare, and for the stylish literary recording of it come together in the archaeology—a testament to a gifted, enigmatic but troubled man. In later years, he was never able to completely shake off his role in the Arab Revolt, or the Lawrence of Arabia legend that had formed around him and which made him a heroic figure so earnestly acclaimed and desired in the post-war years. He was ashamed by the treatment of Feisal and the Arabs at the Paris Peace Conference after the war and sought peaceful anonymity mostly as lowly Aircraftsman Shaw in the Royal Airforce. He refused medals from King George V, and influential positions, observing later simply that 'The war elevated me too high'.

Bedouins waiting for water distribution
in the south of what was then Palestine,
July 1917

101

Bedouin women during water distribution in southern Palestine, July 1917

Laying a water pipeline across the desert, 1915. Water supply was one of the most crucial elements in facilitating warfare in the Middle East.

Catching locusts in Palestine during the terrible locust plague, June 1915

A street scene in Damascus, c. 1915–16

Crowds fill the walls of Damascus at a public event, c. 1915–16. On 6 May 1916, Djemal Pasha simultaneously executed seven Arabs in Damascus and fourteen in Beirut for alleged anti-Turkish activities.

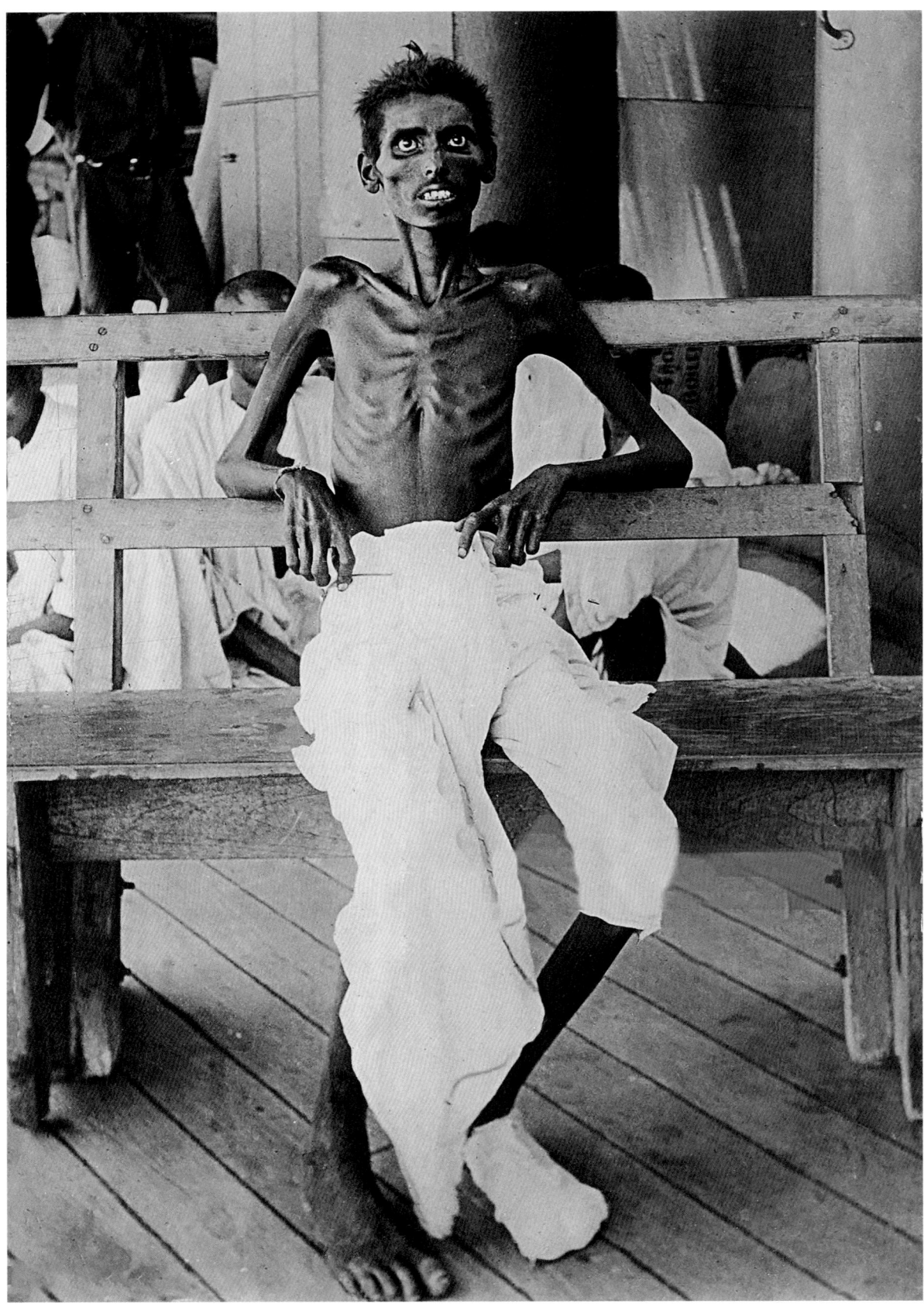

An Indian soldier after the British surrender at Kut Al-Amara on 29 April 1916. Some 13,000 men of the British Indian garrison were sent to Anatolia on what were literally death marches. More than half died of exhaustion, deprivation, or disease.

During the Armenian Genocide, thousands of people died in death marches: an Armenian man surveys human remains in the desert of Deir ez-Zor (Syria).

Survivors of the genocide: Armenian women at a loom at the shelter in Ghazir, Lebanon, 1920

Children who survived the Armenian Genocide in the playground of the orphanage in the American colony in Jerusalem, late 1918

Greek Orthodox refugees from Samsun (Turkey) have arrived in Patras (Greece), whence they will be evacuated by railway wagon to the Greek interior in the aftermath of the population exchange between Greece and Turkey (as provided for in the Treaty of Lausanne), 1923.

An orphaned Armenian boy, survivor of the genocide, c. 1921

Russian soldiers stranded on the Gallipoli peninsula, possibly fleeing the civil war in Russia, 1922

Greek Orthodox refugees from Asia Minor, 1922. Hundreds of thousands of people were displaced during the Turkish War of Independence (1920–1922).

Greek Orthodox refugees during the distribution of soup on the island of Chios, where they were stranded after fleeing Smyrna, late 1922

Official portrait of
Mustafa Kemal Atatürk

King Hussein of the Hejaz in Amman during a visit to his son, King Abdullah of Transjordan, January 1924. Hussein, who was promised a large, independent Arab kingdom by the British in 1915, was left empty-handed after the war.

Prince Faisal (sitting in chair) surrounded by officers, c. 1920

T. E. Lawrence—aka Lawrence of Arabia—in typical Arab dress

121

The surrender of Jerusalem, 9 December 1917. British troops pose with captured Ottoman soldiers and with civilians, including Mayor Hussein Salim Al-Husseini (with walking stick and cigarette).

Prince Abdullah (1882–1951) was the second son of Sharif Hussein of the Hejaz. In 1921 the British placed him on the throne of their Transjordan Mandate.

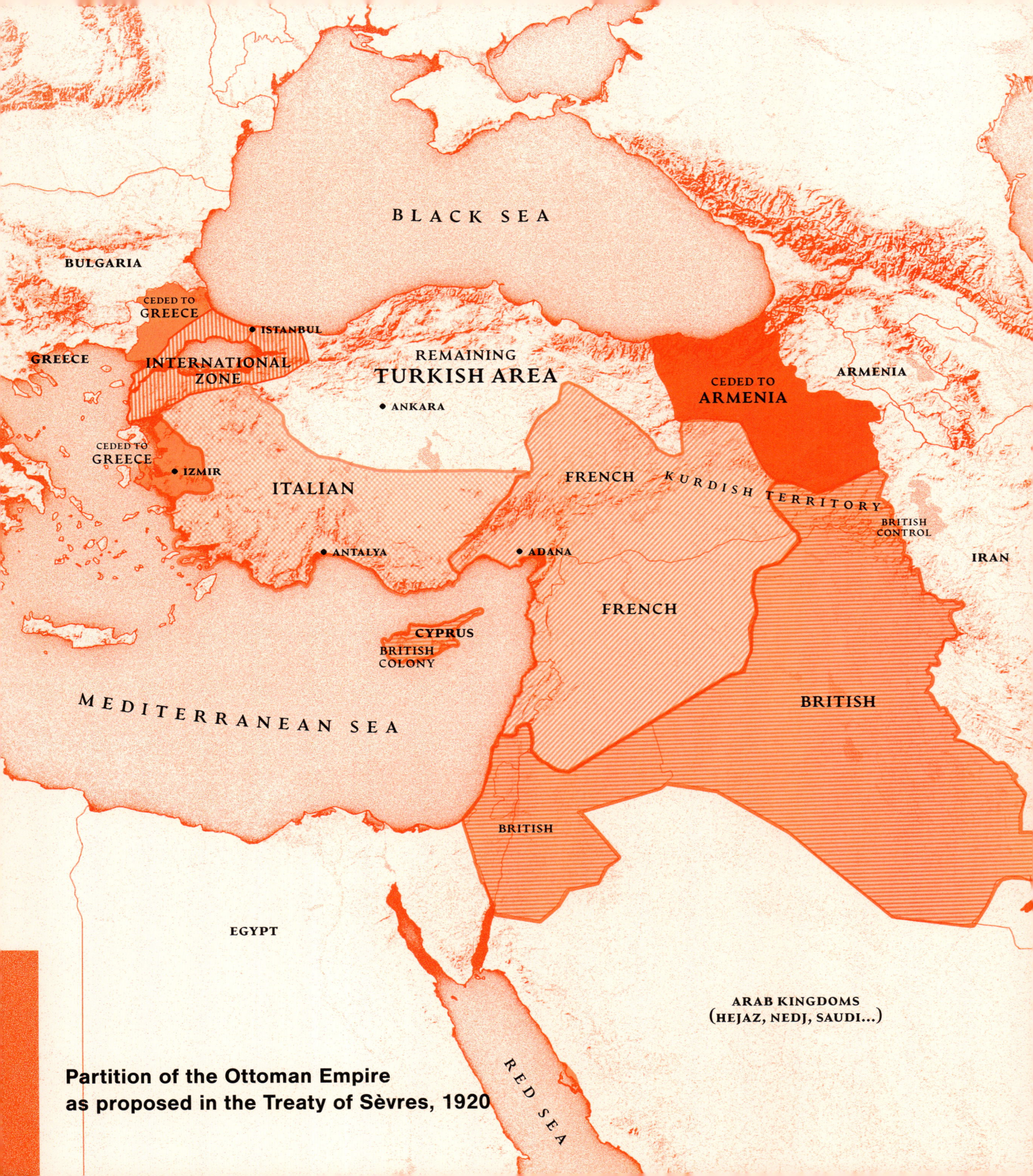

Ozan OZAVCI

Sèvres, Lausanne, and the Invention of the Middle East

Conventional wisdom holds that the First World War came to an end in the autumn of 1918. Exhausted in battles and overhauled by revolution, the Central Powers called for an armistice in October. This was the prelude to the five peace treaties that were eventually signed between the Allied Powers and the defeated during the Paris Conference of 1919–20. Each settlement was concluded in a different suburb of the French capital.

Paris Peace Treaties of 1919–20

TREATY	SIGNATORIES
Treaty of Versailles 28 June 1919	Germany and the Allied Powers
Treaty of Saint-Germain 10 September 1919	Austria and the Allied Powers
Treaty of Neuilly 27 November 1919	Bulgaria and the Allied Powers
Treaty of Trianon 4 June 1920	Hungary and the Allied Powers
Treaty of Sèvres 10 August 1920	Ottoman Empire and the Allied Powers

The last of these accords took place in the exhibition room of the Manufacture nationale de Sèvres and addressed the future of what had been the Ottoman Empire, a region now known as the Middle East. Like the other four, Sèvres was a punitive treaty. It espoused the Wilsonian principle of self-determination selectively, re-drawing the borders and partitioning the dominions of the Ottoman Empire. New polities emerged from a crucible of inter-imperial rivalry, competing business interests, and Christian visions of the 'Holy Land'. The treaty partly de-imperialised Asia Minor by paving the way for the establishment of an independent Armenia (Article 88) and by including vague pledges to establish a Kurdish 'national home' as well. At the same time, it re-colonised formerly Ottoman lands in Mesopotamia and along eastern Mediterranean coasts, carving out new states under British (Iraq, Transjordan, and Palestine) and French (Syria and Lebanon) control.

During the conferences in London (February–April 1920) and San Remo (April 1920) at which the articles of the Treaty of Sèvres were negotiated, France and Britain had largely agreed on how to share Mesopotamian oil. Even though the Sykes-Picot Agreement of 1916 had assigned the oil-rich province of Mosul to the French, in 1920 France ceded it to British-controlled Iraq. Borders were re-drawn in line with the Great Powers' oil and other strategic interests. Future pipelines connecting Mesopotamia to the Eastern Mediterranean were considered, above and beyond the French desire to oust the defiant King Faisal from Damascus and control the Levantine coasts. Unlike Britain, France had never made hasty promises to support Arab, Jewish, or any other community's claims to a territory of their own. Her foreign policy focus lay elsewhere, in keeping

A map presented by T. E. Lawrence to the British war cabinet in November 1918 as a recommendation for the partitioning of the Ottoman Empire. Lawrence's view was clearly pro-Arab and questioned the fate of the Kurds in the Mosul region.

Germany weak for as long as possible. France's network of business interests and French Roman Catholic missionary institutions in the region nonetheless needed protecting.

In 1922, the League of Nations sanctioned the mandate system in the territories conceded by the Ottoman Empire, which was classified by the diplomats of the time as Class A mandates next to the Class B and C mandates in Africa and the Pacific islands. The overarching discourse was to supervise these Class A polities to liberation and civilisation after centuries long oppression under the Ottoman Empire. Everybody knew, however, that this was a fig leaf for Anglo-French imperial aspirations. As early as 1920, an uprising took place in Iraq to defy the new international (dis)order, only to be brutally suppressed by the British Royal Air Force.

The term 'Middle East' had been coined at the turn of the twentieth century by American and British naval strategists. It was now adopted as a semantic and geostrategic category in the sense familiar to us today. An extremely diverse body of peoples (Arabs, Kurds, Turcomans, Shiites, Sunnis, Alawites, Druzes, Yazidis, Assyrians, Jews, etc.) suddenly found themselves tucked into new, artificial, European-controlled states whose borders had been drawn—often in a straight line—far away, in Paris. The kink in the Transjordanian-Iraqi border even came to be called 'Churchill's sneeze', indicating the apparently casual spirit in which the region was partitioned by the stroke of a distant minister's pen. Egypt remained under British influence. Nominally it emerged as an independent state under King Fuad and later his son King Farouk. As with Iraq, Iran, and (almost) Jordan, Egypt's puppet monarchy would eventually be ousted from power in the 1950s.

Like the other Paris treaties, Sèvres left deep scars in the political psyche of the vanquished. It triggered what the Dutch historian Erik-Jan Zürcher calls 'a legacy of revanchism'. But unlike the other four treaties, Sèvres was never ratified. At least in the Ottoman Middle East, the First World War was not entirely over yet. It had only changed form.

After the autumn of 1918, the Great War was 'decentred', to borrow from the American historian Jay Winter. Its final phase lasted longer in the Middle East than in many other parts of the world. This was in large measure a result of the emergence of a Turkish nationalist resistance movement against the provisions of the Mudros Ceasefire of October 1918. The British occupation of Istanbul (13 November 1918) and the French invasion of Cilicia (17 November 1918) sparked piecemeal, regional defiance of national forces (*kuvâ-yı milliye*) confronting European armies of occupation. The landing of the British-backed Greek troops in Smyrna/Izmir in May 1919 further galvanised the Turkish nationalists, which steadily rallied around a senior officer named Mustafa Kemal Pasha.

In February 1920, the last Ottoman parliament proclaimed a National Pact denouncing and defying territorial partition of the empire by the Allied Powers. This parliament was soon dissolved by the British forces, however, and what remained of the empire was still ruled

Romanticised depiction of Mustafa Kemal Atatürk's entry into Smyrna (Izmir) following the Turkish victory during the Turkish War of Independence, late 1922

by Sultan Mehmed Vahdettin and his cabinet—both under British sway. Mustafa Kemal's nationalist movement swiftly responded to the dissolution of the Istanbul parliament by promulgating a new assembly on 23 April 1920—in Ankara, a nondescript dusty town deep within the Anatolian heartland.

By the time the Treaty of Sèvres was signed, therefore, there were two governments in Turkey: the Sultan's in Istanbul and Kemal Pasha's in Ankara. Neither was prepared to accept the newly signed treaty. The Sultan and his heirs Prince Selim and Abdul Halim were of the belief it would reduce the Ottoman Empire to 'insignificance and powerlessness.' Despite immense foreign pressure, Mehmed's cabinet refused to ratify it. This meant that, other than the majority of artificial borders in the so-called Arab world it determined, Sèvres was stillborn.

Differences among the Allied Powers, particularly among Britain, France, and Italy, also played a considerable role in this shift. At the London and San Remo conferences in 1920, they had assigned Smyrna/Izmir to Greece. But both France and Italy were uneasy with this decision, fearing that it would fan further confrontation and violence in Asia Minor. Exhausted by war and massively in debt, neither of them desired to engage in a prolonged armed confrontation with Turkish nationalist forces. Not that they were not happy to let the Greeks 'enforce' Sèvres. But the priority of both Paris and Rome was to advance their economic and financial interests in the post-war Ottoman Empire. As early as 20 October 1921, France and Mustafa Kemal's government signed the Treaty of Ankara, also known as the Franklin-Bouillon Treaty, following the ignominious retreat of French forces from Cilicia (in southwest Anatolia) that spring. To the dismay of her allies, Paris unilaterally recognised the new Kemalist regime.

In October 1920 a Barbary macaque bit King Alexander of Greece; the wound became infected and proved fatal. After this bizarre incident, Constantine once again ascended to the throne. The return of the popular king prompted the electoral defeat of his adversary Prime Minister Eleftherios Venizelos in November. It was Venizelos who had initiated Greek foreign policy on the premises of the irredentist 'Great Idea' (Megali Idea), which called for Hellenic expansionism in Asia Minor. It was Venizelos's influence on British Prime Minister Lloyd George which led him to support the Greek invasion of western Anatolia. A seasoned statesman, Venizelos was well aware that the Megali Idea could not be realised without the approval of the other Great Powers. After landing Greek troops in Smyrna in May 1919, he had therefore followed a cautious policy. His fall from power upended Athens' stance. Incoming Prime Minister Dimitrios Gounaris launched a risky offensive deep into the Anatolian heartland, seeking to capture Ankara and break Mustafa Kemal's forces.

As Venizelos anticipated, this demarche clashed with Italian interests, jeopardising as it did Rome's sphere of influence as well as her economic plans. The Italians saw in Gounaris's expedition a breach of the 1920 agreements with Britain and Greece at San Remo and Paris. The Italians

Greek soldiers in action during the Graeco-Turkish War of 1919–1922, which left Greece the loser.

accordingly terminated their occupation of Antalya (Adalia, on the southwestern coast of Anatolia) and its environs in August 1921, having mended relations with the Ankara government earlier in the year.

The conflict between Greek and Turkish armies continued until September 1922. The battles in Sakarya (August–September 1921) and Dumlupınar (August 1922) determined the outcome of the war: resounding defeat of the Greek forces. As the Greeks retreated to Izmir and the Aegean coast, they adopted a scorched-earth policy, partly out of vengeance but also seeking to slow down their Turkish pursuers. In early September, the Hellenic forces' occupation of Smyrna/Izmir came to an end. At once a dreadful fire broke out in the Greek and Armenian quarters of the town, mostly likely a brutal Turkish retaliation for the invasion. The fire swept away a sizable portion of this once booming metropolis on the Aegean, pushing thousands to seek refuge on European ships. The events have gone down in Greek history as 'The Catastrophe'. Prime Minister and king paid a heavy price. In September 1922, Gounaris was executed by the Revolutionary Committee. King Constantine abdicated.

Several hundred kilometres to the north, Turkish nationalist forces came toe-to-toe with British forces occupying the Straits, notably at Chanak (Çanakkale). Faced with the prospect of going back to war, Conservative members of the British parliament turned on their leader, Lloyd George, driving him from office. On 11 October 1922, the Mudanya Ceasefire ended the Chanak Crisis. A decade after the 'Greater War' began in the region, peace was finally within sight. A new peace treaty was needed. Lausanne in Switzerland was chosen as meeting place.

Although peace had broken out in Europe four years before, at Lausanne the wounds of battle, the refugee crisis, and the psychological scars were fresh for Greeks and Turks. A new peace was to be negotiated between the victors of 1914–18 and the victors of 1919–22. The conference was opened on 20 November at the Casino de Montbenon and lasted until 24 July 1923, with a short interruption (4 February–24 April 1923). The negotiations were grouped under three headings, 'Territorial and Military Questions', 'Regime of Foreigners', and 'Economic and Financial Questions', most of which were resolved by the end of the conference.

For the Turkish nationalists, represented by Ismet (Inonu) Pasha, the ultimate objective was to undo Sèvres and ensure Turkish sovereignty in the territories claimed under the National Pact of 1920. They looked to 'Turkify' Asia Minor, eliminating all 'foreign elements', by which they meant non-Muslims. The Greek delegation led by Venizelos recognised that the security of fellow Greeks remaining within Turkey could no longer be guaranteed. Under the terms of a convention signed in January 1923, an unprecedented population exchange was agreed upon. About one million Greek inhabitants of Asia Minor and half a million Muslims resident in Greece were forced to leave their homes for a new life. Far from being welcomed 'home', many former Ottoman Greeks found a chilly reception within Greece, and were viewed with suspicion by 'fellow Greeks'.

Of all territorial issues, the Mosul question proved to be the most challenging. The National Pact of the Turkish nationalists claimed Mosul as part of the emerging new Turkey. Even though the Turks were ready to forsake some of their territorial claims in Thrace and the Aegean Islands, Mosul's oil reserves gave it vital importance. This was exactly why Britain also grasped it tightly, insisting that it was part of the British mandate of Iraq. Vague promises of access to Mosul's oil by Inonu succeeded in breaking the Allied front at Lausanne. The 'Mosul Question' was left to the League of Nations to decide. Only in 1926 would Turkey abandon its claims to Mosul in return for a share of the royalties.

Unlike the Paris Conference of 1919–20, the Armenians and the Kurds were not given formal accreditation in Lausanne. An Armenian delegation was actually present on the shores of the Lake Geneva to defend their national interests and ensure an Armenian National Home in Asia Minor. Their position initially seemed strong. Thanks to a shared Christian faith, disgust at the 1915 Armenian Genocide, and a powerful diaspora in western Europe as well as the United States, the Armenians had plenty of popular support among the Allied Powers. But it was a victors' peace, and the Turks knew it. The Turkish delegation was therefore adamant in its rejection of Armenian claims. They did not even allow the 'Armenian issue' to be discussed officially. As the first article in Ismet Pasha's instructions from Ankara commanded, it was 'out of question'.

In the end, Sèvres was torn up and Lausanne shaped the future of the new Middle East. Neither an Armenian nor a Kurdish state would ever emerge in Asia Minor. The Armenian and Assyrian genocides (or 'massacres' as they were known at the time) were swept under the carpet as if they had never happened. War exhaustion meant war crimes were forgotten. As with the Mosul question, the defunct Ottoman Empire's sovereign debt, the Straits, and the border between Turkey and Syria were all left unaddressed. Desperation for peace prevailed.

Signed on 24 July 1923, the Treaty of Lausanne was the last of the peace settlements at the end of the First World War. It is the only one still in force. In Turkey, Lausanne is considered the birth certificate of the new republic that was promulgated three months later, on 29 October 1923. Yet for nearly a century now its clauses, and the lands given and taken at Lausanne—especially Mosul—have been an object of heated debates, providing ample fodder for political opportunists seeking to polarise opinion. The discussions of the early 1920s are still very much alive in Turkey. For Armenians and Kurds, Sèvres remains the great hope betrayed at Lausanne. An increasing number of historians argue that the First World War ended not in 1918, but in 1923. But it was only the official end date. Needless to say, for many Middle Easterners, it continues to this day.

Halide EDIB

1884–1964

In 1919 it was not only Paris that saw arguing, lobbying, and fighting for autonomy and self-government. Wherever the war had created a power vacuum, groups of people were claiming their right to self-determination. In Turkey, it was this that motivated Halide Edib, a Turkish nationalist writer, feminist, and professor, to take to the barricades. There are many aspects to Halide's story, which is both complex and controversial.

Part of elite Ottoman society, Halide had enjoyed a privileged upbringing. Her Turkish nationalist convictions developed during the Balkan Wars of 1912 and 1913, when she worked as a nurse at the front. She witnessed the massacres of Ottoman Muslims living in the Balkans. As she commented later in her memoirs:

> 'The Turkish Moslem massacres in the Balkans did not arouse one quarter of the indignation which the Armenian massacres had done ... I believe the two different measures meted out by Europe to the Moslem Turks and to the Christian peoples in Turkey keenly intensified nationalism in Turkey. They also aroused the feeling that in order to avoid being exterminated the Turks must exterminate others.'

On several occasions both during and after the war, Halide criticised the genocide of the Armenians. Yet in 1916 and 1917, she ran a home in Lebanon where Armenian and Kurdish orphans were forced to convert to Islam. Some saw that compulsory Islamisation (or 'Turkification') simply as a device that would save a great number of children from a worse fate, but to many Armenians it made her complicit in the Armenian Genocide.

In 1918 and 1919, Halide gave fiery speeches denouncing the Allies' aggressive policy on Ottoman territory and campaigned for the preservation of Turkish sovereignty. She had her own ideas about what constituted nationalism, believing that it should emerge from below, from the people, not be imposed from above. Nationalism ought to lead to a more humane concept of love and justice, not to feelings of military or cultural superiority. In 1919, in one of her most famous speeches, she said in this context:

> 'Governments are our enemies, peoples are our friends, and the just revolt of our hearts our strength.'

As Mustafa Kemal Atatürk's interpretation of nationalism became ever more authoritarian, she found herself increasingly at odds with the policy. In 1926 she fled to Europe with her husband.

Halide Edib during one of her rousing speeches

Top: Children of Turkish Muslims from Thessaloniki during the Balkan Wars, 1912. Bottom: Armenian children after the genocide, 1919.

Prince Faisal (centre) at the Paris Peace Conference, July 1919. In the second row, from left to right: Faisal's advisors Rustum Haidar and Nuri al-Said; Capt. Pisani, a French liaison officer; T. E. Lawrence (wearing an Arab headdress), his British liaison officer; and Tahsin Qadri, Faisal's military attaché. The man at the back is unidentified.

Elizabeth F. THOMPSON

The Arab Liberal Revolutions of 1919 and the Violent Consequences of European Suppression

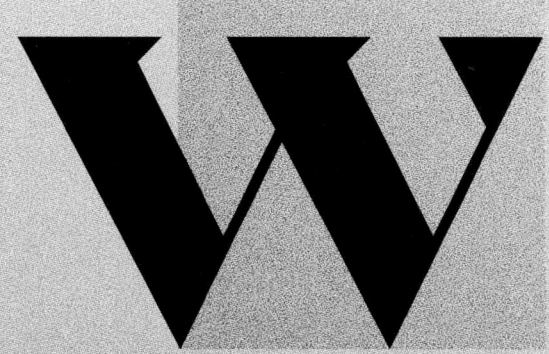

When Europeans cheered their armistice on 11 November 1918, Arabs of the defeated Ottoman Empire were already mobilising to secure their rightful place in a new world made safe for democracy, as proclaimed American President Woodrow Wilson. Since 1916 Arabs had waged a revolt against the Ottoman military dictatorship, which had caused their peoples much suffering during the First World War. In early October, the Arab army entered Damascus and declared an Arab constitutional regime. In Egypt, which was detached from the Ottoman empire in 1914 when Britain declared a protectorate, political leaders also took up Wilson's promises to demand independence. Like the Turks in Greater Syria, the British had drained the Egyptian population of the most basic resources for livelihoods even as they had forced one million peasants into Allied labour brigades.

By 1919, revolution filled the air across the formerly Ottoman Arab world. Their revolution was aimed not against the West, but rather to demand inclusion among the civilised nations that had supported the Allies in fighting for democracy. The most popular and powerful politicians in Greater Syria (including today's Syria, Lebanon, Palestine/Israel, and Jordan) promoted liberal constitutional government and the rights of Arabs within a new world order governed by international law and the League of Nations. By embracing East-West unity and equality under the umbrella of the Paris Peace Conference, Arabs aimed to overturn nineteenth-century racial and colonial hierarchies.

The sole independent Arab state recognised at Paris in 1919 was the Kingdom of the Hejaz, governed by Sharif Hussein of Mecca. He had launched the anti-Ottoman revolt on the basis of a promise by the British that Arabs in Greater Syria would also gain independence after the war. In June 1919, Sharif Hussein's representatives therefore signed the Treaty of Versailles, which brought the League of Nations into existence and promised provisional independence for Greater Syria and Iraq under a temporary League mandate. The League, in Arab eyes, had been the brainchild of Woodrow Wilson, whose Fourteen Points had opposed colonial gains in the war and promised autonomy and self-determination to the peoples of the Ottoman Empire.

But the ink on the Versailles treaty had barely dried when Allied leaders initiated a counter-revolution against Arab independence. In Paris and at the League's headquarters in Geneva, colonialists made false claims that Arabs were not liberal or modern enough to rule themselves, and that they were fanatical Muslims who would oppress and even massacre non-Muslims in their societies. By using military force to occupy Greater Syria and Iraq, Britain and France violated the League's requirement that mandates be established only with Arab consent. Likewise, in Egypt, the British turned machine guns on civilians who protested the prolongation of their protectorate.

The story of how the Allies betrayed Wilson's principles to expand their colonial empires has been told before, but only in terms of how they denied Arabs independent

Sheikh Rashid Rida, a prominent Islamic reformer, president of the Syrian Congress in 1920, and publisher of the widely read magazine *The Lighthouse* (*al-Manar*)

American President Woodrow Wilson

states. Far more was at stake: the future of democracy and human rights in the entire Arabic-speaking region. After the First World War, Arab politicians sincerely believed in the universality of liberal principles: that all peoples had equal rights to freedom and self-governance. They demonstrated that commitment in the democratic policies they promoted in their own societies. But by the time the last peace treaty was signed in 1923, Arabs had been relegated to the status of colonial subjects, stripped of basic human rights under international law. Arabs in Greater Syria did not even have the right to petition the League of Nations. In their humiliation and disillusion, we may discern the roots of violence and anti-Western hostility—and the enduring weakness of democracy—in Arab politics over the last century.

Arab Aspirations for Dignity, Equality, and Self-Government

On 11 November 1918, Prince Faisal gave a victorious speech in the northern Syrian city of Aleppo. Faisal had served in the Ottoman parliament before the war and maintained contact with Syrian opposition in the early years of the war. Arab politicians had rejoiced at the 1908 revolution, which restored the Ottoman constitution after years of tyranny. They advocated greater local autonomy for the Arab provinces. But after a military coup in 1913 and the plunge of empire into total war, they turned against Ottoman rulers who in 1915 massacred Armenians, sending refugees into Syria, and who continued to confiscate grain when drought and famine struck. A half-million people died from famine in Greater Syria. Then, in 1916, the Ottoman governor of Syria executed the best and brightest of Arab political leaders on suspicion of treason. At that point, Faisal joined the revolt as the leader of the northern Arab army, which fought against the Ottomans alongside British forces in a campaign later made famous by T. E. Lawrence and the movie *Lawrence of Arabia*.

When Faisal's army entered Damascus in early October 1918, Greater Syria lay in ruins. Entire forests had been cut down to fuel Ottoman railroads, farms lay fallow because the army had confiscated animals and tools and recruited all able-bodied males. Millions of women waited in vain for their fathers, husbands, and sons to return from the battlefront. One out of four recruits would never return: the Ottoman casualty rate exceeded that of most European belligerents in the First World War.

Never again would Arabs submit to such brutal military rule. Politicians determined not only to revive the constitution of 1908 but to revise it to prevent such tyranny. With the support of Muslim and non-Muslim leaders in Syria, Faisal proclaimed a constitutional government for all of Greater Syria. Syrian Arabs who had previously served as military officers, governors, bureaucrats, lawyers, and scholars under the Ottoman regime rallied to build the new Syrian state, which they intended to be federated with Sharif Hussein's kingdom in Arabia and an independent state in Iraq. Like their counterparts in the lands of defeated Russian and Austro-Hungarian empires, they viewed the war as a revolution against the tyranny of emperors and for government by the people.

In jubilation on November 11, Faisal read to his audience a declaration made by Britain and France a few days earlier, promising 'liberation of the peoples so long oppressed by the Turks and the establishment of governments and administrations deriving their authority from the initiative and the free choice of native populations.' By the summer of 1919, Syrians would elect a congress to draft a constitution. While almost half of the delegates came from territory of what is today Syria, most delegates came from what is now Lebanon, Palestine/Israel, Jordan, and Turkey.

Two days later in Cairo, on November 13, Saad Zaghlul led a delegation of prominent politicians to petition the British Resident, Sir Reginald Wingate, for permission

Left: Saad Zaghlul, leader of the Egyptian Wafd Party who inspired the 1919 Revolution

Right: The memory of Saad Zaghlul was revived in this graffiti, drawn on a wall in Cairo in 2012. Zaghlul is raising his middle finger at the military junta, saying 'It's no use, sons of bitches'.

to travel to Europe so that they might submit their own plan for independence. Before the war, Zaghlul had served as a cabinet minister under the British, who had occupied Egypt in 1882. Zaghlul's delegation contended that Egypt's wartime sacrifices had earned it the right to independence. However, against the advice of a Belgian judicial advisor who warned of mass protests, Wingate denied the delegation permission to travel. Like Gandhi in India, Zaghlul turned to popular pressure, inspiring a revolt against British colonialism in early 1919. 'The right to life and liberty can no longer be confined to certain continents or certain latitudes,' Zaghlul declared.

Just a stone's throw from Zaghlul's house, another post-war leader worked in his publishing office to prepare a special issue of his magazine in praise of Woodrow Wilson's revolutionary vision to base peace on self-determination of all nations. The magazine was *The Lighthouse*, read by reform-minded Muslims from Morocco to Indonesia. The publisher was Sheikh Rashid Rida, a native of Syria exiled in Egypt twenty years earlier for opposing the Ottoman sultan's tyranny as a violation of Islamic principles. In the December 1918 issue of *The Lighthouse*, Rida called Wilson a spokesman for God who promised that 'the interest of the weakest is as sacred as the interest of the strongest' and that the rights of small nations even outside of Europe will be guaranteed in the peace. Immediately after publishing this issue, Rida and other Syrian exiles formed the Syrian Union Party (SUP) to draft a constitution for independent Syria. Britain stalled their visas, but they managed to travel to Syria the following summer.

Arabs had good reason to hope that Woodrow Wilson might help them to avoid the Allies' plan for colonial occupation. American troops had sealed the Allied victory and the capitals of Europe welcomed Wilson with parades and banners as the 'Champion of the Rights of Man'. January 1919, Prince Faisal had travelled to Paris and met personally with Wilson. In his formal presentation to the peace conference, the prince argued that Arabs were as civilized and prepared for self-government as the Poles, Czechs, and Serbs who had already begun to carve their own nation-states out of the defeated Austro-Hungarian empire. 'I ask you not to demean this [Arab] nation that has truly served civilisation,' Faisal concluded.

Wilson applauded the speech and later organised a committee of inquiry to poll Syrians on their political preferences. Syrians elected a congress that declared the independence of the Syrian Arab Kingdom in March 1920, after Faisal's further negotiations in Paris failed to win recognition of their sovereignty. Under Rashid Rida's leadership, the congress drafted a democratic constitution that disestablished Islam as the state religion and guaranteed absolute equality among Muslim and non-Muslim citizens. It remains the most democratic constitution ever drafted in the Arab world.

Fighting as brothers-in-arms with the Allies between 1914 and 1918 had inspired a revolutionary belief that Arabs might find their rightful place in a new, liberal world order. They shared the hope of Japanese delegates to Paris, who proposed that the new League of Nations guarantee equality of all races under international law. Arab leaders similarly promised equality within their own societies: Syria's 1920 constitution and the Egyptian Wafd party both declared equality between Muslims and non-Muslims.

The Colonial Denial of Arab Rights at the Paris Peace Conference

The Paris Peace Conference rejected the Japanese proposal on racial equality, and to no one's surprise, launched a counter-revolutionary effort to expand colonial empire. Unity among the Allies in the First World War had been cemented by mutual promises of colonial expansion as a

Leaders of the 1920 Syrian Congress with King Faisal (centre). Rashid Rida is pictured at the top right. He was one of several religious men in congress who wore turbans. Tribal sheikhs wearing scarves and former Ottoman bureaucrats, wearing tarbooshes, were also prominent in the congress. Younger nationalists tended to eschew headgear.

reward for victory against the Central Powers. Most notably, in the 1916 Sykes-Picot Agreement, France, Britain, and Russia outlined a plan to divide Syria, Mesopotamia, and parts of Turkey among themselves.

The first Arab country to face colonial counter-revolution was Egypt. In March 1919, the British arrested Saad Zaghlul and members of his new Wafd (Delegation) Party who had persisted in stoking popular support for independence and constitutional government. In response to the arrests, demonstrations flooded Cairo's streets declaring a revolution against Britain. Strikes and protests spread across Egypt, led by civil servants, students, workers and peasants. A popular song scolded the British for wartime theft and ingratitude.

> 'Pardon us, Wingate! But our country has had enough! You took our camels, donkeys, barley, and wheat aplenty. Now leave us alone!'

Muslim and Christian religious leaders joined the protests to promote cross-sectarian unity and equality in an independent Egypt. Prominent women led delegations to foreign embassies. Like women in Syria, they joined this revolutionary moment to promote equality among the sexes. 'Send our message to America and to President Wilson personally,' one of their petitions demanded. 'We believe they will not suffer Liberty to be crushed in Egypt, that human Liberty for which you[r] brave and noble sons have died.'

The British responded to the 1919 Egyptian Revolution with violence; shooting hundreds of unarmed civilians dead and burning entire villages. They agreed to release Zaghlul and his fellow Wafdists only after securing Wilson's support for the continued protectorate. Protests continued into 1920 and 1921 as the British Colonial Minister Alfred Milner stonewalled negotiations with Zaghlul.

Egypt became a microcosm of the battle between colonial paternalism and the revolutionary new world order based on law and rights. 'The failure of the Zaghlul-Milner talks was the failure of a dialogue between an Empire and a nation in the process of revolutionary birth,' a historian remarked. In the end, the British unilaterally decreed partial independence for Egypt in 1922, reserving full control of military and foreign affairs to themselves. Zaghlul was elected prime minister but under a constitution written in his absence that severely curtailed the power of parliament.

Meanwhile, in late 1919, pressure to respect the self-determination of Arabs disappeared after Woodrow Wilson's stroke and the American Congress's refusal to ratify the Versailles treaty. In April 1920, Britain and France convened the Allies at San Remo to impose their mandates by force. The French sent tanks, airplanes, and colonial troops to occupy Damascus in July 1920. Faisal and the congress fled into exile. The British imposed their mandate on Palestine, despite Arab protests against the mandate's promise to establish a Jewish homeland there. The British also imposed a mandate on Iraq, which rose up in armed revolt in the summer of 1920. For Syrians and Iraqis, the bitterness of being stripped of their rights was especially acute: They had been citizens of a sovereign state in 1914 and had fought in support of the Allied democratic cause since 1916.

Consequences of Counter-Revolution

In 1921, still bearing his title as President of the Syrian Congress, Rashid Rida travelled to the Geneva to warn the president of the League of Nations assembly against humiliating liberal Muslims:

> 'It does not befit the honour of this League, which President Wilson proposed to include all civilised nations for the good of all human beings ... for it to be used as a

Women demonstrating against the British protectorate, March 1919

tool by two colonial states. These states seek to use this Assembly to guarantee, in the name of a mandate, the subjugation of peoples ... If the Balkans were the spark of war in the West, then Syria, Palestine will ignite the fires of war in both the West and the East.'

The League ignored his and others' warnings and ratified the French and British mandates in 1922. The mandates entered international law in 1923 following the Treaty of Lausanne, the last peace treaty signed after the First World War. Soon afterward, the British forced the popularly elected Saad Zaghlul to step down as prime minister in Egypt. In the eyes of Arabs—and other colonial peoples who aided the Allies, like Indians and Africans, the League of Nations became a colonial instrument of oppression, not the guarantor of human rights.

The repercussions of the Allies' counter-revolution rippled through the twentieth century, obliterating memory of the brief democratic dawn after the First World War. It also reversed aspirations of unity, instead opening a chasm between East and West. 'Islam' and 'liberalism' became opposing concepts in Arab politics. After 1923, Rida lost hope in the League and began preaching the need for Muslims to find a separate justice in Islam. In 1928, his student, Hasan al-Banna, founded the Muslim Brotherhood upon the idea that Islamic justice opposed Western liberalism. Many Syrians also lost faith in liberalism as an expression of Muslim values. Islamists opposed liberal politicians who had supported the 1920 Congress and constitution as traitors and collaborators with the West. They would unite to form the Syrian Muslim Brotherhood in the 1940s. In both countries, the Brotherhood supported constitutions in the later twentieth century that re-introduced Islam as the basis of legislation, against the belief in 1919–20 in equality regardless of religion.

Only in the 2011 Arab Spring would popular movements calling for 'bread and dignity' attempt to revive the cross-sectarian, liberal democracy that the Arab world had enjoyed briefly after the First World War. These young activists and a new generation of historians is now recovering a history that may inspire new democratic movements in the future.

Pedestrians and a horse-drawn carriage on the Galata Bridge, which spans the Golden Horn at Eminönü, with minarets and mosques visible in the background. Istanbul, Turkey, c. 1900.

Australian and New Zealand troops lugging equipment on the beaches of Anzac Cove, where they landed with difficulty on 25 April 1915, Gallipoli, Turkey

Jerusalem, view of the Jaffa Gate,
14 December 1917

A group from the Egyptian Camel Transport Corps passes over the Mount of Olives, East Jerusalem, Palestine, 1918

British occupation troops had to keep order as tensions grew between Jewish newcomers and the native population. Checkpoints appeared in various places and passers-by were randomly searched for weapons. Jerusalem, Palestine, 1920

An anti-Zionist demonstration moves through the city. The assurances of the Balfour Declaration were in direct contradiction to the promises Britain had previously made to Arab nationalists. A British colonel tries to calm the crowd. Jerusalem, Palestine, spring 1920

British occupation troops outside the walls of the holy city. On 25 April 1920, at the San Remo Conference, Britain received a mandate for Palestine, which was approved by the League of Nations on 24 July 1922. Jerusalem, Palestine, April 1920

View of the Jewish Quarter in Jerusalem, Palestine, late 1918

The British willingly deployed their Royal Air Force to control Iraqi mandate territory and quell uprisings.

View of a street in Baghdad, Mesopotamia (Iraq). The San Remo Conference (25 April 1920) also envisioned a British Mandate for Mesopotamia. Despite the protests, the British founded the new state of Iraq and installed Prince Faisal as king in 1921.

Prince Faisal inspects British Indian troops, Haifa, Palestine, spring 1920. At the time, Faisal was still working on the founding of the Arab Kingdom of Syria, which would incorporate Palestine, Lebanon, and parts of Syria and Transjordan.

Top: French barricade in the streets of Damascus, Syria, during the fighting with Faisal's troops. Bottom: Burning houses and ruined buildings after French bombing. France refused to recognise the Arab Kingdom of Syria under Faisal and in the summer of 1920 invaded Syria and Lebanon to claim the territories, in accordance with the Sykes-Picot Agreement.

Ceremonies held in March 1921 in Jerusalem, Palestine, to mark the inauguration of Prince Abdullah as king of Transjordan, established as a British mandate in that year. In the centre (between the ladies in white), from left to right: Prince Abdullah bin Ali, Herbert Samuel (the British High Commissioner for Palestine), and Winston Churchill (then Secretary of State for the Colonies).

150

Prince Faisal, later king of Iraq, arrives at St Pancras station, London, c. 1920.

El-Salt (present-day As-Salt, Jordan) 20 August 1921. The local population listens to the declaration of the British High Commissioner Herbert Samuel following the foundation of Transjordan.

Istanbul, Turkey, 1921. 'Street children of different denominations' (including a Turkish, Russian, Greek, and Jewish child, according to the original caption) 'form an army that begs for money and work in the busiest and most expensive city of the moment'.

A woman and child, Istanbul, Turkey,
sometime between 1915 and 1923

Scenes from a refugee camp set up among the ruins of the Temple of Hephaistos, Athens, Greece, 1922. Hundreds of thousands of people fled during the Turkish War of Independence (1920–1922). Moreover, the terms of the Treaty of Lausanne (1923) called for a 'population exchange': as of 1923 Greece had to take in more than a million Orthodox Christian refugees from the former Ottoman Empire.

April 1920, Mount Scopus in Jerusalem, Palestine: children decorate the graves of British servicemen who fell during the campaigns in Palestine (1917–18). The Jerusalem British War Cemetery, which also contains the graves of servicemen from the British Commonwealth, was established on this site in the 1920s.

Bruce SCATES

Victor and Vanquished: Contested War Memory in the Middle East

Before the Great War, the Ottoman Empire extended the length and breadth of the Middle East. Though its authority was often fragile and contested, Constantinople claimed control over much of region. With the war's end, that Empire was in ruins and victorious Allied Powers divided the spoils between them. It is within that framework—the geopolitical reality of victor and vanquished—that commemoration of the war dead in the Middle East must be set.

Recovering and interring the bodies of the fallen was the first commemorative imperative all combatant nations faced. This task was particularly pressing in the case of the British forces (including Dominion troops from South Africa, Newfoundland, Australia, and New Zealand and a massive colonial contingent raised in India). Driven by the protocols of the Imperial War Graves Commission (IWGC), the British Empire vowed to identify as many of the war dead as possible, bury each man as near as practical to where he 'fell' and safeguard that grave in perpetuity. This was a dramatic departure from previous commemorative practice. To memorialise the war dead as individuals and to assert (through uniform graves and careful protocols of naming) what was often touted as the 'equality' of remembrance, was almost unprecedented. Prior to the First World War, statues were raised to victorious generals; the men they commanded were often buried *en masse* and unidentified, particularly if those troops were recruited from the periphery of Empire. In the Middle East, as in every other theatre of the Great War, massive cities of the dead rose on the site of former battlefields, and major hospitals were soon flanked by graveyards.

To mark and maintain a grave involved an assertion of ownership. That proved a simple enough matter in territories mandated to the Allies. The inscription set on the entrance to Imperial War Cemeteries in Egypt and Palestine is telling. 'This land was granted in perpetuity'. 'Granted' was hardly appropriate. After little or no consultation with local communities, the British extended pre-existing graveyards or created new ones.

By far the most significant land grab took place at Gallipoli. The campaign in the Dardanelles was a disastrous defeat for the Allies. Throughout 1915, it claimed the lives of over 20,000 British troops, 10,000 French (including African colonial forces), 1300 Indians (including Sikhs, Hindus, and Muslim) and over 10,000 Anzacs (an expeditionary force raised from the British dominions of Australia and New Zealand). Unlike Egypt, Palestine, and Syria, where a mobile war scattered the war dead across vast areas of desert, fighting on the Gallipoli Peninsula was confined to three clearly defined sectors, Helles to the South, Suvla to the North, and a tiny beachhead in between where Australian and New Zealand troops first landed in April. Establishing war cemeteries in the last of these places—promptly dubbed Anzac by the men who served there—shaped yet another set of new commemorative protocols and long delayed the settlement of any permanent peace with Turkey.

From the outset, the governments of Australia and New Zealand rejected calls to relocate their war dead to large concentration cemeteries (as was the practice at Suvla and Helles and elsewhere throughout the Middle East). Rather, the men should be left 'where they fell so that the site of their graves, scattered across the rugged terrain, would 'mark their heroism'. With many bodies never found,

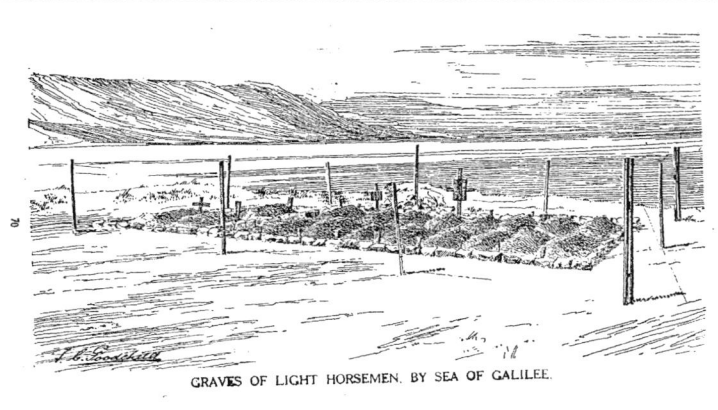

Sketch of a battlefield cemetery with the graves of Australian Light Horsemen, Galilee, Palestine. The mobile war scattered the war dead across vast areas of desert. Sketches like these were intended to console distant families in Australia.

the IWGC deemed it best to treat the entire Anzac area as 'one great cemetery'. John Burnet's design stipulated each graveyard be walled on three sides only—a refusal to demarcate or compartmentalise sacred ground. Anzac became one vast memorial complex, every ridge, gully, and outpost harnessed in a dramatic gesture of remembrance.

The Turks reluctantly conceded ownership of French and British war cemeteries as part of their post-war settlement with the Allies. But this demand (as one Turkish official put it) 'to consecrate entire battlefields' went considerably further. It would carve out an 'Anzac estate' from the same ground where tens of thousands of Ottoman soldiers were buried, and compromise Turkish control over the strategically important heights of the peninsula. The clause remained a sticking point over months of fraught negotiation; Lord Curzon, leader of the British negotiating team, described it 'as haggling over the bodies of the dead'. But the Gallipoli campaign, Australia and New Zealand's first major military engagement of the Great War, and both nations' baptism of fire, was already a cornerstone of national identity. Fears that the 'heathen Turk' might desecrate the Anzac's distant graves hardened the Dominions' resolution. Article 144 of the Treaty of Lausanne formalised the Empire's claim over Anzac, a compact seen nowhere else in the Middle East, nor for that matter any other theatre of war.

The graves of the war dead were marked in different ways by different nations. French graves at Helles, one of the largest concentrations of that nation's war dead in the Middle East, were marked with star pickets. A durable, economic, and inventive mode of commemoration, this repurposed war material was originally used for barbed wire entanglements. Christians might read the shape as a cross; Muslims (the faith of many Senegalese troops) were assured this was a secular rendering of the fleur-de-lis. Unlike the British, the French made no pretence of any equality in remembrance. Officers are entombed in handsome stone tombs on the heights of Morto Bay cemetery; the troops they commanded set out in neat rows beneath them. Remains that could not be identified were gathered in ossuaries, long a feature of French funeral architecture. Each plot is known to entomb several thousand bodies, a pile of whitening bones amassing anonymity.

From Egypt to Syria, British graves in the Middle East look much the same as they do on the Somme or Flanders. A white upright tombstone displays the badge of the regiment, records name and rank, and carries (in many cases) an epitaph chosen by next-of-kin. The last was the IWGC's most significant point of departure from its cherished principle of uniformity and allowed the bereaved some point of individual connection with graves few could ever visit. Christian graves are distinguished by the bar relief of a cross; others bear the Star of David. The headstones of Indian troops were also 'appropriately marked'. All but the smallest graveyards feature the Commission's standard monumental signatures, the Stone of Remembrance (non-denominational and akin at once to cenotaph and altar), and a tall, finely proportioned cross. With a bronze sword attached to its face, the latter could be seen as a symbol of martial valour rather than an exclusively Christian symbol, addressing a range of religious convictions held across the British Empire

On the Western Front, British war cemeteries were often likened to parish graveyards, clean white stone set on soft green lawn and bordered by colourful flower beds. In the Middle East, that illusion was much harder to sustain. Desert winds eroded the deepest inscriptions, necessitating continuous and costly maintenance. Corrosive soil necessitated the abandonment of graveyards in Palestine. All but the hardiest of plantings perished.

'Recumbent plaques set on concrete pillars': an alternative mode of marking the graves of the war dead. Note the sturdy oak framing this graveyard. Plantings like this were a way of reclaiming some corner of a foreign field as home. Even so families continue to lobby for the repatriation of Gallipoli's bodies, fearful graves might be desecrated. While the French repatriated some bodies from the Dardanelles, British authorities refused all such requests, asserting the state's jurisdiction over the bodies of the war dead.

As in so many other ways, Gallipoli's graves posed an anomaly. Recumbent plaques set on concrete pillars were deemed more stable than upright tombstones in a region prone to earthquake. No crosses of sacrifice were raised; the authorities feared both the theft of saleable bronze and the desecration of overt Christian symbolism. Valiant efforts were made to plant out the Anzac Battlefields with Eucalypt and Rimu, and seedlings raised in the Kew Gardens carefully transported to the Peninsula. All succumbed to the rigours of a bitter winter, as did many of the troops buried there.

In contrast to these lavish protocols of remembrance, Ottoman troops were hurriedly buried in (for the most part) unmarked graves. The mobile nature of fighting in the Middle East, the stretching of supply lines, and ever pressing military priorities militated against commemoration in war time. After the war, the Ottoman Empire surrendered four-fifths of its former territories, and with it the graves of their war dead. Ironically, some of the best-preserved Ottoman graves of the Great War are those of Turkish prisoners who died in British hospitals. Though many such plots are nameless, they are cared for in perpetuity by the War Graves Commission.

Gallipoli, site of the most significant Ottoman victory of the war, offered little more scope for remembrance. Turkish losses were colossal, more than twice that of the Allies. Anzac war graves detachments garrisoned on the Peninsula spent much of their time 'tidying up' the battlefield, a euphemism for gathering up the bleaching bones of former enemies and burying them far from the gaze of grieving pilgrims and intrepid travellers. Occupying forces found few actual graves but appear to have respected those they did. To this day, the tomb of Sergeant Mehmet can be seen near the battlefield of the Nek, the place where Ottoman and Anzac forces collided in 1915. It is only in recent years that the Turkish government has embarked on any substantial commemoration of the war dead. This takes the form of what might be called surrogate cemeteries, marking the site of where massed Ottoman graves may once have been located and pointedly aligned with the manicured cemeteries established by the War Graves Commission. The symbolism of this late twentieth-century commemoration is compelling. At Anzac, a cemetery dedicated to the memory of the 57th Regiment (cut down to a man, it is claimed) includes a stylised pyramid, signifying a martyr's ascent to heaven. At Helles, acres of ground are dotted with glass tombstones, bearing the names of men drawn from the furthest reaches of the Ottoman Empire. Modern Turkish commemoration thus serves diverse and sometimes conflicting imperatives; secular adulation for Turkey's post-war leader, Ataturk (himself a key figure in the Gallipoli campaign), Islamic zeal for what is presented as a holy war against the Infidel, and the pan-Ottoman narrative now ascendant in Erdoğan's Turkey.

Marking actual graves was one matter, raising centralised monuments another. Many of these, particularly those raised by the British, serve the principal purpose of memorials to the missing. Driven by the logic of its charter, the War Graves Commission set about recording each man's name in stone, either at cemeteries or on centrally located battlefield memorials. An 'imposing monument' at Helles was one of the first such structures to be completed. Its central feature is a great pillar, honouring the naval armada that attempted to force the narrows. Around it is a series of stone panels, groaning with the names of some 20,000 men lost on the Peninsula or buried at sea. Shining white by day, and with lights sweeping the sea at night, it was intended to be seen by every ship traversing the Dardanelles. A memorial to the lost also proclaimed dominion. Not to be outdone, the French raised a lesser tower at the highest point of the Morto Bay cemetery, astutely exploiting geography.

'Claiming the landscape' with imposing monuments to highlight the sacrifice of the nation's heroes and frame the official narrative

Left: The New Zealand Memorial to the Missing, perched near the summit of Chunuk Bair, Gallipoli

Right: A French Memorial raised near Ismailia in Egypt to commemorate the defense of the canal

Just as they rejected centralised graveyards for the dead, the British Dominions of Australia and New Zealand insisted on their own separate memorials to the missing. Both these national memorials were located on key features of the Anzac Battlefields: Lone Pine represented the furthest reach of the Australian advance; Chunuk Bair, the highest point of the Peninsula originally taken by New Zealanders. Fashioned from the same white stone used at Helles (and, purportedly, the building of Troy) these sites boast commanding views of Allied and Ottoman trench lines. The latter was designed to catch the sun from every angle, a mass of stone and concrete broad and high enough to be seen by every ship en route to Constantinople. Commemorative architecture thus achieved the purest of ironic inversions: swallowed up by the earth, the missing now mastered the landscape.

The Turks for their part raised few battlefield memorials. And—in this place of hotly contested commemoration—those they did were not long tolerated by the Allies. A simple marble obelisk marking the Turkish defence of Lone Pine was destroyed to make way for the Anzacs' largest cemetery. In a rather pointed gesture, shards of the shattered stone were sold to raise funds for crippled soldiers. Again, it is only in recent years that the Turks have raised new memorials, proclaiming their possession of the only substantial battlefield of the First World War still in their control. A massive monument, festooned with Turkish flags, dwarfs the original allied memorials at Helles; a statue to Atatürk stares down New Zealand's pylon on Chunuk Bair, and, on the site of the landing, his words welcoming 'grieving mothers from far away lands' speak the new commemorative language of friendship and reconciliation.

Memorials to the missing might appear to express IWGC's commitment to equality in commemoration. In fact, the opposite was often the case. It was not just that men with no known grave had no chance of an individual epitaph, or that the numbing columns of nameless names subsumed the individuality of the war dead. The War Graves Commission was ever mindful of the need for commemorative economies and doubted many Indian families would make a pilgrimage to the Middle East. Accordingly, the memorial at Port Twefik in Egypt honouring some 4000 Indian dead from Sinai and Palestine who had no known grave, recorded their names in memorial registers rather than in stone. A similar practice disenfranchised the dead from the Mesopotamia campaign. Over 32,000 Indian troops were commemorated by number alone in Basra. In recent years, the Commonwealth War Graves Commission has raised supplementary memorials across the Middle East, correcting what it admits was the Eurocentric bias of commemoration. But there is little prospect of ever retrieving the names of those who served 'under the banner of Empire' in the Egyptian Labour Corps and Camel Transport Corps. A Special Committee commissioned to review historical inequalities in commemoration estimated as many as 50,000 were denied any meaningful or lasting memorial. The same is true of over 200 unnamed Singaporean casualties of the Chinese Labour Corps.

The Turkish memorial to Ottoman Troops killed at Lone Pine not long before its destruction by the War Graves Detachment. Whilst the (few) Turkish private graves were usually respected, this symbol of martial valour, circled by murderous artillery shells, was not. Gallipoli remains one of the most contested commemorative landscapes in the Middle East.

This essay has explored contested and unequal commemoration across the Middle East. In closing, it might be noted that the campaigns in Egypt, Palestine, Sinai, Mesopotamia, and Gallipoli were not just commemorated in the lands in which they fought. The names of such places were etched deep on memorials raised in India and Australia, France, Britain, and New Zealand. And, in one case at least, a monument from these now oft-forgotten campaigns made an extraordinary passage from one side of the globe to the other. In 1932, Australia raised a memorial to the men of the Desert Mounted Corps on the shores of the Suez. It took the form of an Australian and a New Zealand soldier steadying their horses in one of the last great cavalry charges of the twentieth century. In 1956, Arab nationalists destroyed the memorial at the height of the Suez Crisis, a counter-commemoration challenging the waning authority of the British in the Middle East. What remained of the statue was reinstated in the grounds of the Australian War Memorial, a relic embodying the contestation of war memory.

George KNOX

1881–1916

In April 2003, shortly after the invasion of Iraq during the Second Gulf War, British Lieutenant Rob Williams accidentally discovered the burial place of his great-grandfather, Charles Williams. He was interred in the neglected Basra War Cemetery. Charles succumbed to dysentery on 7 November 1916, during the British campaign in what was then Mesopotamia. In that one moment, eighty-seven years of fraught history were captured: Iraq, where Charles died, was 'created' as a country by British mandate in the aftermath of the Great War. That controversial construction ignited conflicts and tensions that continued to fester until 2003 and beyond. Hence, Rob's presence as a member of a Western intervention force was also controversial.

After the First World War, the Basra War Cemetery became the final resting place of 2,490 Commonwealth servicemen. The bodies of 40,641 casualties of the Mesopotamia campaigns were never recovered. The Basra Memorial was erected to commemorate them, with an accompanying register of names. One name that is not to be found in the register is that of the Londoner George Knox. Born on 11 September 1881, Knox was in business in the City in early 1914. Shortly after war broke out, he took up a commission in the 8th Battalion of the Royal Lancaster Regiment and spent the following year in England undergoing intensive training. George had hoped to see action at the front in France, but in January 1916 he was suddenly attached to the 6th Battalion of the Royal Lancasters, which was sent to Mesopotamia.

In Mesopotamia, George's unit was deployed to Kut al-Amara (Al-Kut, Iraq), where the British Indian Army garrison had been cut off and was under siege by Ottoman forces. Knox was killed on 9 April 1916 during one of the many attempts to relieve the town (all of which failed). His body was never found. And his name also went missing in the administrative whirligig of the Imperial War Graves Commission. The British war graves service thought he was still serving with the 8th Royal Lancaster Battalion, which was in Flanders at the time of his death. This is why George Knox is commemorated on the Menin Gate in Ypres, even though he never set foot in the Westhoek.

Portrait of George Knox

A stonecutter chisels names into the panels of the Menin Gate Memorial to the Missing in Ypres, dedicated to the soldiers of the Commonwealth armies killed in the Ypres Salient whose graves are unknown. George Knox's name can be found on panel 12, although Knox never set foot in Flanders Fields. Photograph by Antony, 1927.

Lord Arthur Balfour meets a cheering Jewish crowd in Tel Aviv, Palestine, when he visits in April 1925 on the occasion of the inauguration of the Hebrew University of Jerusalem.

Dotan HALEVY

The First World War and the Zionist-Palestinian Conflict, 1914–1948

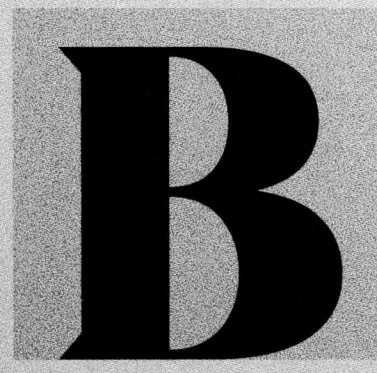

By the outbreak of the First World War, the majority Arab population in Palestine and the settler society of European Jews, which had established itself in the land since 1882, had already been embroiled in an open political conflict. The Jewish settler society was rather small, numbering some 20,000–25,000 (out of some 60,000 Jews throughout the land) compared to the Arab majority of some 700,000. However, enjoying European protection, foreign capital, and wilful disregard of the Ottoman authorities, this community was quite resourceful. By 1914, it had already purchased some 400,000 dunams of agricultural land and established national institutions which conducted the communities' civil affairs somewhat independently of the Ottoman state and separately from the native Arab population. The Palestinian press, religious leadership, and political representatives were explicit about the imminent danger to peaceful life in Palestine posed by what increasingly came to be understood as the Zionist project. Violent clashes on the ground erupted every so often around the question of labour and land in the Jewish colonies and the country's primary cities. Zionist activity aimed at enlarging enclaves of exclusive Jewish hegemony and economy (the *Yishuv*) also threatened to disrupt longstanding relations between the native Jews of the country, Sephardi and Orthodox-Ashkenazi alike, and the local Arab majority.

However, under the conditions of war, these tensions seemed to have lessened. The land of Palestine had strategic significance for the Ottoman Empire. Bordering Sinai, it was a launching pad for assaulting the Suez Canal, a move intended to regain the Ottoman province of Egypt, which came under British occupation in 1882. To concentrate troops for such an ambitious campaign, the Ottoman army extended the Empire's railway system in Palestine, laying two routes to the southern towns of Gaza and Beersheba on the edge of the Palestine desert (later known as the Negev or *Naqab*). The Ottoman governor of greater Syria and commander of the Ottoman fourth army, Djemal Pasha, also took advantage of wartime conditions to rapidly execute modernisation projects in country's principal cities, paving boulevards and laying infrastructure to manifest imperial grandeur to the civilian population. Yet the civilian experience of this imperial interest was one of heavy distress. The Ottoman troops encamped in Palestine relied on the land's supply of foodstuffs and material resources. This entailed ongoing seizures of civil property, which was confiscated from the local population to serve the army—from pack animals, carts, engines, and fuel, to land, buildings, and forests. Thousands of men were enlisted in the Ottoman military, reducing the country's agricultural capacity and economic resilience, while British and French

Anti-Zionist demonstration at the Damascus Gate, Jerusalem, Palestine, 8 March 1920

blockades in the Mediterranean prevented supplies, people, and information from reaching Palestine. In 1915, these hardships were compounded by unprecedented waves of locusts that raided agricultural fields. With working hands and resources already diminished, the civilian population could barely withstand this additional environmental havoc. The result was an ongoing famine which caused thousands to perish, as well as a general sense of isolation and uncertainty as to future political developments.

The Great War was felt in Palestine through its effect on civilian lives more than through actual fighting in the country's limited battlegrounds. The exception to this rule was mainly experienced by the Arab population of southern Palestine with the arrival of British troops there in 1917. Following the failed Ottoman attempt to strike the British at the Suez Canal and break into Egypt in 1915, the British Egyptian Expeditionary Force (EEF) started its advance toward Palestine through the Sinai desert. By January 1917, the EEF reached the gates of Palestine near the town of Rafah and entrenched its troops in preparation for an onslaught on the Ottoman defence line between Gaza and Beersheba.

Foreseeing an impending attack, Djemal Pasha ordered the evacuation of the civil population of Gaza, the third largest city in Palestine after Jerusalem and Jaffa, in early March 1917. Some 40,000 people were forced by the Ottoman military authorities to relocate anywhere from Jaffa all the way to Aleppo before the fighting started. The British tried to enter Palestine through Gaza twice in March and April 1917, employing tanks and gas bombs for the first time in the Middle Eastern theatre. But the Ottoman defence proved impregnable. In the months that followed, each party on the Gaza front retrenched itself, refreshed troops, and changed command. No face-to-face fighting took place, yet both sides suffered under heavy bombardment from gunships, airplanes, and artillery.

Beyond the heavy military casualties, these long months of trench warfare spelled disaster for Gaza and its agricultural hinterland. The combination of fortification and shelling caused the urban fabric of the city to disintegrate. Ahead of the third, and eventually victorious, British offensive on 7 November 1917, Gaza suffered another round of heavy bombardment—this time as part of a feint by General Edmond Allenby, who led the EEF's main effort to the town of Beersheba instead. The result of these months of trench warfare was the massive destruction of the entire Gaza region. It was the single most disastrous battleground in Palestine and arguably in the Middle East as a whole. Following the war's end, it took some two decades for the war-torn region to recover its former populace and economy. Some of the people evacuated from the city never found reason to return.

Wartime hardships pushed Jews and Arabs alike to set aside their political aspirations and concentrate on survival. With the outbreak of the war, representatives of the Sephardi Jewish community in Jerusalem, where a version of Ottoman patriotism developed alongside firm belief in Zionist ideology, even planned to join forces with prominent Muslim notables to initiate a mechanism of mutual Jewish-Arab support. As the war dragged on, however, European Zionist leaders that managed to gain material support from the United States gradually marginalised the Sephardi elite's role in leading the Jewish community in Palestine, thereby thwarting initiatives of this kind.

For the most part, then, Jews and Arabs became dependent primarily on political dictates from above. Seeking to recover realms of sovereignty lost to European imperial domination, the Ottoman administration cancelled the economic and legal privileges granted to foreign institutions and nationals and obliged them to naturalise as Ottoman citizens or leave the country. Zionist Jews, who often enjoyed foreign protection, thus came under direct threat. Such acts signalled to the Arab majority that wartime measures might deal a fatal blow to Zionist colonisation.

Zionists in Palestine and abroad understood the Ottoman measures similarly, and the *Yishuv* members became anxious to maintain at the very least what had been achieved thus far. They took the Ottoman authorities' forcible deportation of several hundred Jewish residents who refused to Ottomanize, and the restrictions placed on Zionist activity by the authorities, as clear signs of malicious Ottoman plans. More than any event, however, it was the forced evacuation of Jaffa and Tel Aviv in late March 1917 that worried Zionist leadership. The Ottoman evacuation order was given to Jews and Arabs alike in anticipation of the impending British invasion. Yet here the Arab population managed to circumvent the Ottoman order—in contrast to the case of Gaza—by relying on the imperative to maintain agricultural production for the Ottoman war effort. As the British assault in Gaza also failed later that month, the Ottoman authorities decided to overlook Arab disobedience. Concerned with showing unequivocal loyalty and subservience to the Ottoman military authorities, however, the 9,000 Jews of Jaffa and Tel-Aviv organised an orchestrated exodus and spread between Jewish colonies across the country. While perceived in Jewish collective memory as a punitive Ottoman act against Zionist society, Ottoman documentation released in recent years proves the contrary. Despite loathing Zionist colonial aspirations, the Ottoman military authorities did not try to extinguish the *Yishuv*, either here or elsewhere. As in Gaza, Djemal Pasha was mainly concerned with removing the burden of caring for civilian matters from the shoulders of the military authorities in potential battlegrounds.

To be sure, the Ottoman general did prosecute and deport people at will, but not on a collective level. Thirty-two men accused of Arab separatism and collaboration with Britain and France were hanged in Beirut and Damascus, including prominent Palestinian notables such as Gaza's former mufti, Ahmad 'Arif al-Husseini. Seventy-one others were sentenced to death *in absentia*. Two thousand families associated with them were expelled from Palestine and Syria to Anatolia, among whom was the famous Palestinian publisher 'Isa al-'Isa, or were incarcerated at the Damascus jail, like the renowned Palestinian pedagogue and author Khalil al-Sakakini. Key figures of the *Yishuv* leadership, most notably David Ben Gurion and Yizhaq Ben Zvi, were deported from Palestine to Istanbul for political reasons. But the only place where deadly measures were taken against Jews in Palestine was in the Ottoman campaign against the British-supported Jewish underground NILI in September 1917.

The Ottoman administration's unequal treatment of Arab and Jews emanated in part from international concern for the fate of the Jewish *Yishuv*. Yet, at the same time, the Ottoman military authority also prioritised the Arab and Jewish cases differently. Arab disloyalty could potentially have developed into a strategic problem, as was in the case of the Arab Revolt led by Prince Faisal of the Hejaz. Arab nationalist thinking started to develop counter to the Empire's Ottomanization efforts prior to the war, and with the outbreak of the Arab Revolt against the Ottomans in 1916, Prince Faisal emerged as the ultimate Arab national leader—indeed, some Palestinians followed him. By comparison, Zionist potential to influence the course of the war through national separatism was negligible.

Wartime conditions thus created similar, even if not comparable, challenges for both Jews and Arabs in Palestine, while Ottoman policies were not designed to change the balance of power between the two groups dramatically. Out of this wartime stalemate, however, a major shift was brewing. To understand how it came about, it is crucial to recall that under the Ottomans, Palestine was

Left: Jewish colony on the plain at Rephaim, Palestine, not far from Jerusalem

Right: Chaim Weizmann, a key figure in the Zionist movement and later Israel's first president after its founding in 1948

not a standalone political unit but a variously defined geographical entity loosely conceived as a place of symbolic significance. Palestine was a sacred space acknowledged by Muslims, Christians, and Jews and had been recognised as a historical territory since biblical times. An Ottoman handbook circulated among military officers under the title of *Filastin Risalesi* roughly defined the boundaries and characteristics of the land that linked together a geographical space encompassing the independent district of Jerusalem, declared in 1874, and the southern part of the province of Beirut. Palestine's fate during the war was inseparable from that of greater Syria, and Ottoman policies towards the emerging national conflict over the land were enmeshed within the broader concerns of Jewish minority rights within the Empire, immigration policies, and the advancement and loyalty of the Arab provinces.

The Zionist-Palestinian conflict moved into a new phase as part of the processes by which Palestine was carved out of its former Ottoman space. Starting November 1917, with the British advance through the Gaza-Beersheba line, Ottoman rule in greater Syria—which had lasted four centuries— rapidly crumbled. In December 1917, the British army took Jerusalem, and by October 1918, it entered Damascus, establishing on its path a military administration to replace the Ottoman authorities. The 1919 Paris peace conference determined the status of the former Arab provinces of the Ottoman Empire as international mandates under the aegis of the League of Nations. At the conference of San Remo in April 1920, the mandate territories were officially divided between Britain and France along the lines of the wartime agreement between the two from May 1916, known as the Sykes-Picot Agreement. Britain established civilian rule over Palestine starting in July 1920, and two years later, in July 1922, the General Assembly of the League of Nations approved the British mandate edict, thus making Palestine an internationally recognised political entity.

While the other Arab provinces of the Ottoman Empire became the British and French mandates of Syria, Lebanon, and Iraq, Palestine stood out because of the political arrangements ushered in by the British. It was the only mandate territory where the imperial power also promoted colonisation by immigrant settlers as part of its international commitment. In the same fateful month of November 1917, when British troops advanced into Palestine after taking Gaza and Beersheba, British foreign secretary Arthur Balfour provided Chaim Weizmann of the World Zionist Organization (via Walter Rothschild) with the letter which later became famous as the Balfour Declaration. Behind it stood the British ideological commitment to the Jewish Question in Europe, the longstanding strategic British plan to gain control over Palestine, and most importantly, British wartime need to convince the United States to join the war and Russia to reassert its commitment to the war effort (which had dwindled since the February Revolution) by winning the hearts of their Jewish populations. The declaration committed to using Britain's 'best endeavours' for 'the establishment in Palestine of a national home for the Jewish people' while referring to the native Palestinian population—the majority of inhabitants—solely as 'the non-Jewish communities of Palestine'. The Palestinian population was promised religious and civil rights, but not political ones. Unlike Jews around the world, Palestinians were not seen in the declaration as a 'people'. Moreover, by binding themselves to Zionist aspirations in Palestine, the British also contradicted their commitment in the McMahon-Hussein Correspondence from 1915–16, which stated that the house of Hussein ibn Ali, the Sharif of Mecca and father of Prince Faisal, would rule the Arab lands following the war's end in return for initiating the Arab Revolt. But the enshrinement of the Balfour Declaration in the British mandate edict of 1920 made enhancing Zionist colonisation of Palestine not

Inauguration of the Hebrew University of Jerusalem, with speeches by Arthur Balfour, Herbert Samuel, and Chaim Weizmann, among others, Mount Scopus, Jerusalem, Palestine, 1 April 1925

only the official British policy, but also the policy the League of Nations itself was obliged to secure from 1922 onwards.

In the eyes of Palestinians, the denial of their political rights in their own land by foreign rulers was a forceful rupture with the course of political development ushered in by the 1908 revolution in the Ottoman Empire. As Ottoman subjects, Palestinians enjoyed substantial political liberty and had representatives in the Ottoman parliament. Palestinian participation in the Arab Revolt and later in establishing the short-lived Arab government led by Faisal in Damascus upon the war's end followed the same aspiration. This Arab state, they hoped, would encompass Palestine as 'southern Syria'. These hopes were shattered by the French occupation of Syria in July 1920, parallel to the British establishment of the civil administration mandate in Palestine that same month. For Palestinians, the land that had experienced growing political, economic, and cultural opportunities under the late-Ottoman rule had been cast into the role of a British colony settled by European Jews, in which the highest echelons of Arab representation had become those of municipal and religious administration.

This reality greatly aggravated the conflict between Zionist immigrants favoured by the imperial regime and the native Palestinian population it had marginalised. The material stress that followed the war, the destruction of the former Ottoman political order, and the carving out of new mandate states around them accelerated Palestinians' national identification, providing a clear 'other' in the form of Zionist settlers. Zionist land purchases, dispossession of peasants, and immigration, which now grew with the blessing of British rule, conveyed to Palestinians the message that the mandate terms would eventually turn them into a neglected minority. And thus, the isolated violent clashes between Jews and Arabs prior to the war evolved into a series of deadly periods of fighting afterward, in 1921, 1929, and then during the 1936–9 Great Palestinian Revolt. It was only during the late 1930s, as the League of Nations' international world order showed growing signs of collapsing into a second global conflict, that Britain finally decided to withdraw from its commitment to the Jewish National Home policy and published the 1939 White Paper limiting Jewish immigration and land purchase. By this point, however, the Zionist project had established itself enough to persist despite decreasing British backing and even to resist the new British limitations. The Palestinian population, economically and politically powerless after the brutal British subjugation of the Great Palestinian Revolt, could not independently resist ongoing Zionist settlement and the influx of immigrants escaping the horrors in Europe. The tension that built up following the Second World War, with the British departure from Palestine already in sight, exploded with the approval of the UN 1947 partition plan of Palestine into Jewish and Arab states. The resulting war of 1948, Israel's War of Independence, and the Palestinian Nakba brought about two inseparable outcomes, entangled to this day: the expulsion and flight of some 750,000 Palestinians from their land to become refugees and the foundation of the State of Israel.

Wasif JAWHARIYYEH

1897–1972

In 1914, Palestine was an Ottoman province with around 730,000 inhabitants, of whom 600,000 were Muslims, 80,000 Christians, and c. 50,000 Jews. The land suffered greatly during the First World War, not only as a result of the military offensives in 1917 but also from famine and epidemics. With a view to a post-war division of the Ottoman Empire, the British presented Palestine (or parts of it) to several different parties: to the Arabs according to the Hussein-McMahon Correspondence, the Zionists as stated in the Balfour Declaration, and likewise to the Turks, who would be allowed to keep Palestine if they withdrew from the war, which they did not. Eventually, in 1920, Palestine came to be governed by British mandate.

Wasif Jawhariyyeh, a Palestinian Orthodox Christian, was a key witness to events in Palestine. He was a gifted *oud* player—the *oud* is a short-necked Arabian lute—and had Muslim and Jewish friends. Besides enjoying a distinguished musical career, he also worked for many years as an official in Jerusalem under the British Mandate. Wasif's diaries offer a vibrant picture of evolutions in Palestine between 1908 and 1948. He saw with regret how the Zionist project sowed divisions between Muslims, Christians, and Jews. The fault for that, in his opinion, lay squarely with the British.

> 'We Jerusalemites of the various denominations had always lived like a family during the Ottoman rule, and there was never any difference between a Muslim or a Christian. But when Britain occupied Jerusalem, it tried to sow trouble, particularly among Muslims and Christians.'

In a critical poem, Wasif referred to British Foreign Secretary Arthur Balfour as an 'auctioneer' who had 'sold' the Christians and Muslims of Palestine. In January 1919, the Arab and Zionist leaders, Emir Faisal and Chaim Weizmann, signed an agreement in respect of Arab-Jewish cooperation, though it was largely ineffectual. Between 1919 and 1923, some 40,000 Zionist Jews settled in Palestine. From 1920 onwards, conflicts between Palestinians and Jewish newcomers occurred with increasing frequency.

Wasif considered himself part of the Arab-Palestinian camp, but he looked back with longing to the time when the communities lived together in relative peace, and he made music with Muslims, Christians, and Jews. The partition of Palestine and the declaration of the State of Israel in 1948 brought an end to the British Mandate. Around this time, Wasif became depressed and retired to a monastery in Jericho.

Portrait of Wasif Jawhariyyeh

Anti-Zionist demonstration near the Jaffa Gate, Jerusalem, Palestine, February 1920

Wasif Jawhariyyeh

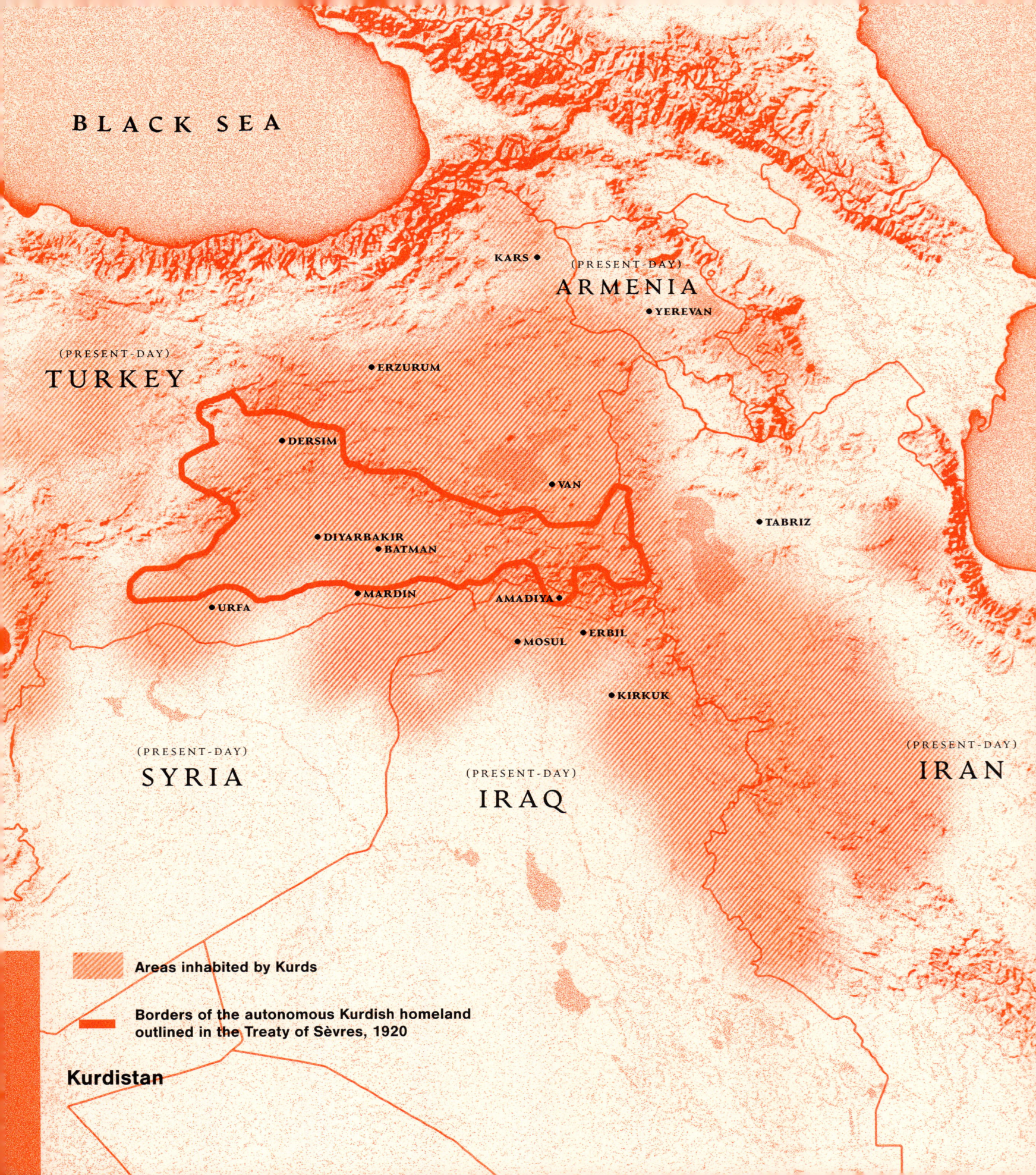

Djene R. BAJALAN

The Kurds and the First World War

The Kurds are a people whose mountainous homeland, Kurdistan ('Land of the Kurds'), today encompasses territories in south-eastern Turkey, northern Syria, north-eastern Iraq, and north-western Iran. They speak a variety of different Indo-European languages and dialects collectively known as Kurdish and share their own unique cultural and historical traditions. Most Kurds adhere to the Sunni branch of Islam, although there are significant minorities of Shi'ites, Alevis, Yezidis, and Yarasan. Moreover, prior to the twentieth century, in many regions, Muslim Kurds lived alongside other ethnic communities, most notably Christian Armenians.

Before 1914, the Ottoman Empire governed most of Kurdistan, with the Iranians laying claim to only the more easterly areas of Kurdish settlement. Historically, the imperial government in Istanbul often had difficulty controlling the Kurds, who were largely organised tribally and who maintained a reputation as a fractious warrior people with little sense of ethnic unity. However, the late nineteenth and early twentieth century witnessed the emergence of a new sense of national consciousness, especially amongst the small but growing Kurdish intellectual elite. Significantly, the early Kurdish movement remained largely pro-Ottoman in its political orientation, although a minority adopted a separatist political stance, most notably Abdürrezzak Bedirhan, who worked with the Ottoman Empire's main antagonist, Tsarist Russia, to ferment rebellion in Kurdistan. However, it was ultimately the outbreak of the First World War in summer 1914 and subsequent Ottoman entry into the conflict on the side of Germany and the Central Powers that would have the most profound impact on the trajectory of Kurdish history.

War and Genocide (1914–1918)

The most immediate effect of the war was that Kurdistan became a frontline in the Empire's struggle against Tsarist Russia. In winter 1914, the Ottomans attempted to seize the initiative, launching an offensive into the Russian Caucasus. However, this ended in disaster at the Battle of Sarıkamış and, over the course of the following year, Russian forces were able to execute an effective counterattack, occupying a vast swath of Ottoman Kurdistan in the process. By early 1916, Russia had taken control of the strategically important cities of Erzurum and Van and advanced as far as the town of Bitlis. The human cost of this conflict was considerable. Kurdish conscripts made up a considerable proportion of the Ottoman military, while Kurdish tribesmen also served as irregulars in the fighting. At the same time, civilian populations were often caught in the middle of the military

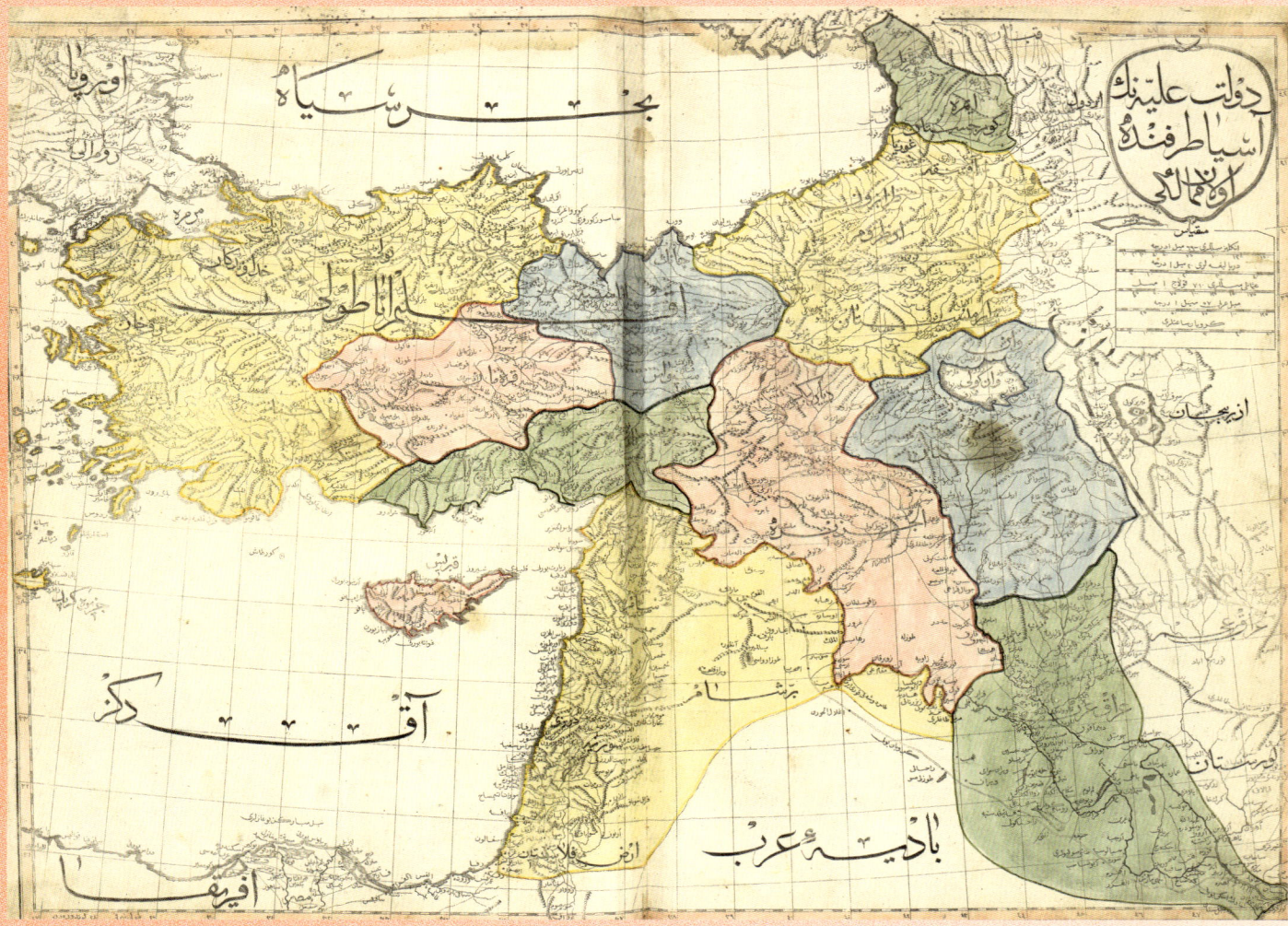

struggle. Although the precise number of Kurdish deaths is difficult to ascertain, Muhammad Emin Zeki Bey, an Ottoman military officer and historian, estimated that some 300,000 Kurds lost their lives during the war.

The suffering was further exacerbated by the policies adopted by the Ottoman government. Following the outbreak of the war, some Ottoman Armenians defected to the advancing Russian army, although the number was relatively small. However, in the aftermath of the Battle of Sarıkamış, the Armenians provided a convenient scapegoat for the defeat. This gave extremist elements of Ottoman leadership the opportunity to 'resolve' the Armenian issue definitively. The outcome was an escalating campaign of genocide that consisted of deportations, rape, and mass killings that resulted in the death and murder of between 800,000 and 1.5 million Armenians. Many Kurds participated in the orgy of violence. However, some sought to protect their Armenian neighbours, leading the government to issue an order that Muslims found doing so would be executed and their homes burned.

More broadly, Kurdish civilians were also the victims of growing Turkish nationalist sentiment amongst the Empire's political elite. Several Ottoman leaders came to regard the salvation of the Empire as being dependent on policies of Turkification. The primary targets of such policies were non-Muslim communities such as the Armenians, but also included efforts to extend the zone of Turkish settlement into Kurdistan. Hence, in 1916, the Ottoman government issued an ordinance on the settlement of refugees that explicitly discriminated against Kurds. Specifically, Kurdish tribes fleeing the fighting were to be disarmed, after which they were to be separated from their leaders, divided into groups of no more than 300, and deported to predominantly Turkish districts in Central Anatolia where they would not constitute more than 5% of the local population. Moreover, while Turkish groups were

Map from the Cedid Atlas, the first Muslim atlas (1803), which situates the distribution of the various population groups in Ottoman Anatolia, Armenia and Syria. The Kurds lived in the mountainous, eastern region, extreme right, colored blue.

Aliser Bey and his wife Zarife Hanim, figureheads of the Koçgiri uprisings that broke out in the eastern part of Sivas province against Mustafa Kemal's regime between 1920 and 1922

allowed to return to their original places of residence, the government denied such permission to Kurds.

Beyond the enormous disruption to Kurdish society brought about by the war, the conflict also had a profound impact on the trajectory of Kurdish political activism. The majority of the Kurdish intellectual elite remained loyal to the Empire, with many serving with distinction in the Ottoman armed forces. However, for Abdürrezzak Bedirhan, the war presented an opportunity. Eager to win Kurdish support for their invasion, the Russians appointed him 'Sultan of the Tribes' and leader of an auxiliary force of pro-Russian Kurds. However, in 1917 the geopolitical situation altered radically with the overthrow of the Tsarist regime in March followed by the Bolsheviks' seizure of power in November. The result was the disintegration of the Russian army. Ottoman forces recaptured the territories that they had lost over the previous two years and, in the summer of 1918, advanced deep into the Russian Caucasus, where they eventually captured and executed Abdürrezzak Bedirhan. Despite their victory on the eastern front, however, Ottoman forces were unable to hold back British offensives in Mesopotamia and Syria and, in October 1918, the Ottoman government requested an armistice. The war was over.

Redrawing the Map (1918–1926)

The capitulation opened the way for a new phase of Kurdish political mobilisation. In November 1918, elites in the Ottoman capital established the Society for the Betterment of Kurdistan (SBK), under the leadership of a veteran Kurdish politician, Sheikh Abdülkadir Efendi. In early 1919, the organisation's leadership approached British officials requesting Kurdish self-government under the auspices of Great Britain. Still, for some within the SBK, this did not preclude a continued connection to the Ottoman state. Indeed, Sheikh Abdülkadir Efendi insisted in the press that Kurds merely sought autonomy under the Ottoman sultan-caliph. However, not everyone shared this position, with many of the group's younger members calling for full national independence. Ongoing disagreements between the SBK's leadership and its more radical members culminated in the formation of a rival organisation in 1920, the Kurdish Society of Social Organization (KSSO).

Despite these divisions, both the SBK and the KSSO continued to lobby the Great Powers—most especially Great Britain—to secure Kurdish national rights. Indeed, the SBK appointed Mehmed Şerif Pasha, a former Ottoman ambassador, as their official representative at the Paris peace conference. Mehmed Şerif Pasha presented Kurdish territorial demands and attempted to reassure the British of the Kurds' positive disposition towards their interests. He also opened negotiations with the Armenian delegation to resolve competing territorial claims. These negotiations proved fruitful, at least in the short term. Mehmed Şerif Pasha came to an agreement with the Armenians over the question of the boundary between Kurdistan and Armenia and, more importantly, the Treaty of Sèvres, signed in August 1920, included provisions pertaining to the formation of an autonomous Kurdish region that would, after a year, have the potential to obtain full independence. Significantly, the Kurdish homeland recognised in the Treaty of Sèvres did not include all Kurdish inhabited districts. Kurdish majority lands to the west of the Euphrates River were excluded, Kurdish inhabited provinces to the east of Lake Van were assigned to Armenia, and the fate of the Kurdish districts in British-occupied Mosul province remained to be determined. Nevertheless, this was an explicit recognition of the Kurds as a nation, one which, at the very least, outlined a pathway to self-government.

However, despite this apparent diplomatic success, events soon conspired to forestall the establishment of the autonomous Kurdish homeland outlined at Sèvres. More specifically, the emergence of resistance to the partition of Anatolia radically altered the realities on the ground. This resistance movement was made up of elements within the Ottoman military and coalesced under the leadership of Mustafa Kemal Pasha (Atatürk) in 1919 following the Greek landing in western Anatolia. The Kemalists rejected the authority of the Istanbul government that had signed Sèvres and founded a rival Ankara-based administration in early 1920. Mustafa Kemal Pasha and his confederates were soon able to establish effective political control over much of what remained of the Ottoman Empire, including most of Ottoman Kurdistan.

The Kemalists' ability to consolidate political power in Kurdish inhabited regions was aided by appeals to Islamic solidarity and fears that an Armenian state would include many heavily Kurdish districts. Indeed, Kurdish fears of Armenian ascendancy were not unfounded, especially given the fact that many Kurds had profited from the genocidal campaigns conducted during the war. Kemalist propagandists also presented those advocating Kurdish statehood as dupes and ne'er-do-wells who would see Kurdistan turned into Armenia. Ankara also acted quickly to repress any attempts to establish Kurdish political organisations in the territories under their control, closing branches of the SBK in Diyarbakir and Siirt in autumn 1919. Thus, by the time Sèvres was signed, Kurdish nationalists had already been effectively excluded from organising in their homeland.

More broadly, the interests of the Great Powers also gravitated against the formation of a Kurdish state. Prior to the First World War, Tsarist Russia had acted as the primary foreign backer of Kurdish nationalism. However, the 1917 Bolshevik Revolution radically altered the geopolitical calculus. The Bolsheviks reversed the traditional anti-Turkish policy of the Tsars, cooperating with the Kemalists at the expense of Great Britain. At the same time, London had little interest in supporting the creation of a Kurdish state. Its primary interests in the Middle East lay in Iraq, which it had occupied during the war. By 1918, British forces had advanced well into the province of Mosul, although the city of Mosul itself was only taken in early November 1918, after the Ottoman capitulation and in violation of the armistice. This brought several important Kurdish districts under British control, most notably the district of Suleimani. Initially, the British appointed an influential local notable, Sheikh Mahmud Berzenci, as Suleimani's governor, but removed him from office in May 1919 after he attempted to assert his independence. In 1922, faced with Kemalist efforts to retake Mosul, the British returned Sheikh Mahmud to Suleimani, but once again he revolted, declaring himself the monarch of an independent Kurdistan. This second revolt was also unsuccessful. Ultimately, British policy in 'Southern Kurdistan' was driven by a desire to stabilise and consolidate control over Mesopotamia, an imperative that served to limit their appetite for Kurdish self-rule. The result was that Britain opted to push for the inclusion of Mosul and its Kurdish subdistricts into the newly formed Kingdom of Iraq rather than support the foundation of a Kurdish statelet in Suleimani.

Thus, Britain had little incentive to intervene further north to secure the Kurdish autonomy outlined at Sèvres. Moreover, the Kemalists military success, culminating with their victory over Greece in 1922, forced a reorientation of British policy. Subsequently, Britain entered direct negotiations with the Kemalists, which resulted in the replacement of Sèvres with a new agreement, the Treaty of Lausanne, signed in July 1923. For Kurdish nationalists,

Sheik Mahmud Barzanji, a Kurdish leader from Suleimaniyah in the present-day Kurdish Autonomous Region of Iraq, who organised several uprisings against the British Mandate in Iraq

Lausanne was a disaster. Not only did it fail to recognise any form of Kurdish self-rule, but it did not even reference the Kurds as a distinct community. Moreover, it set in motion the formalisation of the partition of Ottoman Kurdistan. The end of the First World War had already brought about a *de facto* partition, with Britain occupying the province of Mosul and its Kurdish districts (as well as some Kurdish majority districts that would eventually become part of French controlled Syria), while the Ottomans remained in control of Kurdish inhabited territories further north. Since Britain had occupied Mosul after the October 1918 armistice, its status remained a point of contention, with the Ankara government continuing to lay claim to the province. However, both Britain and the newly formed Republic of Turkey agreed to international arbitration and a subsequent League of Nations commission awarded Mosul to the British-backed Kingdom of Iraq, a decision that was ratified in the 1926 Treaty of Ankara. The map of the Middle East had been redrawn, but the hopes of Kurdish nationalists that the collapse of the Ottoman Empire would bring about a Kurdish state had been dashed.

The Legacy of the First World War and the Middle East's Kurdish Question

The First World War and its aftermath were without doubt defining moments in the history of the Kurdish people. On a most basic level, the war radically altered the demographic order of the land within which the Kurds lived, with the annihilation of the Ottoman Armenian community cementing Kurdish demographic supremacy. Yet, this did not create conditions favourable to Kurdish statehood. While the Ottoman imperium had been dissolved and, in its place, a new regional order of nation-states had come into being, the post-war process of redrawing the map left no space for Kurdish statehood. Instead, by the mid-1920s, Ottoman Kurdistan had been partitioned and the Middle East's Kurdish population found itself as a minority in the nation-states of Turkey, Iraq, Syria, and Iran. Moreover, state elites in Ankara, Baghdad, Damascus, and Tehran increasingly viewed the Kurds as an obstacle to forging a unified national identity. Hence, over the course of the last century, not only have political manifestations of Kurdish identity faced state repression, but so too have relatively benign expressions of Kurdish cultural and linguistic distinctiveness. The outcome of this has been that the relationship between the Kurds and the nation-states within which they reside has often been tense and marred by periodic cycles of violence. Despite perennial Kurdish political and military resistance to this state of affairs, the post-imperial geopolitical order established after the First World War has proved durable and, therefore, the 'Kurdish question' remains very much alive.

Gertrude BELL

1868–1926

Gertrude Bell was a remarkable woman: born in County Durham, England, she would become a world traveller, mountaineer, archaeologist, writer, and wartime head of British intelligence in Mesopotamia. She had a network of contacts in Britain's highest circles, held senior positions in post-war Iraq, and in Baghdad she founded the Iraq Museum, devoted to Mesopotamia's ancient civilisations. She grew up surrounded by rich and powerful men.

Having taken first class honours in history at Oxford, Bell set out to explore the wider world. Between 1900 and 1914 she was involved in several archaeological expeditions to the Middle East. In the autumn of 1915, her knowledge of the languages and geography of the region led to her recruitment into British Intelligence in the Middle East. Having first been assigned to the Arab Bureau in Cairo, in 1916 she was sent to British military headquarters in Basra in Mesopotamia (modern Iraq), where she provided summaries of recent Arab history and reports on British-Arab relations. As the war progressed, she was given increasing powers and responsibilities.

When the war ended, Mesopotamia was mandated to the British in accordance with the Sykes-Picot Agreement. On 23 August 1921, the British established the Kingdom of Iraq. T. E. Lawrence's wartime comrade, Faisal I bin Al-Hussein, who had been recently deposed in Syria, was placed on the Iraq throne. In theory the new state acquired a form of local self-government, but the British were in control of foreign and military affairs, as well as the country's oil-rich areas.

Gertrude Bell occupied some of the top positions in the administration and so played an important role in the whole process. She was closely involved in drawing the borders. The British took full advantage of her knowledge of the region—but that, of course, was also very subjective. Like many imperialists, she was convinced that 'the peoples' who lived there 'were not yet ready to govern themselves'. She also tended to pigeonhole the local populations and to favour one group over another, which led to a good deal of division. For instance, she subjected the Kurds who lived in the oil-rich region between Mosul and Kirkuk to Arab rule in Iraq, whereas the Kurds themselves wanted to be part of an independent Kurdish entity. That 'construction' led to many post-war ethnic and religious tensions that still persist today.

Portrait of Gertrude Bell

Amman, Transjordan. Gertrude Bell was an influential figure in the shaping of the modern Middle East after the First World War. She was present at numerous negotiations and decision-making moments. This photograph, taken at Amman airport in the spring of 1921, shows Bell (centre) in the company of Herbert Samuel, Wyndham Deedes, and Prince Abdullah.

Drilling for oil in one of the Persian oil fields near Abadan (Iran, near the Iraqi border), 1909. The oil fields were managed by the Anglo-Persian Oil Company, a British concern.

Jonathan Conlin Oil: A Crude History of the Great War

Jonathan CONLIN

Oil: A Crude History of the Great War

The story of oil and the Great War is usually told as one in which governments suddenly became aware of the importance of oil to modern warfare and responded by seeking to take control of private oil companies and oil-bearing lands across the globe—particularly lands in the Middle East. 'Control of oil' was achieved by imperialist expansion abroad and by greater economic regulation at home: partial nationalisation of private companies, for example. If only it had been that simple.

Few individuals get to smell crude oil as it gushes from the ground. The same might be said of the many products it contains, from heavy ship oil through gasoline to kerosene, and on to lubricants and the chemicals behind everything from film to TNT. These products powered the dreadnoughts which bottled up the German navy and shelled Gallipoli. They powered the trucks and cars carrying men and materiel to the front lines in France and Belgium, as well as the planes and shells which flew high above the battlefield. Finally, they powered new weapons—notably tanks—which many hoped would end the stalemate of trench warfare. The resulting oil dependence certainly came into focus during the Great War, but it was not a 'lightbulb moment'.

Far from feeling in command, statesmen and diplomats felt uneasy. The war had also seen the oil industry consolidate into a handful of large companies, each with global reach. These were the world's first multi-national companies, a phenomenon familiar to us today, but a source of both wonder and suspicion a century ago. It was difficult to understand how these companies' interests could align with those of individual nations. Alongside the familiar 'Powers' (Britain, France, Italy, the United States), oil seemed to become a 'Power' of its own.

From Baba Gurgur to *Bagdadbahn*

For centuries mankind had exploited and revered the 'eternal flames' caused by seepages of oil and gas. Baba Gurgur ('Daddy Fire') in Mesopotamia (Iraq) is one such natural curiosity. Rubbery pitch was extracted from shallow, hand-dug wells and used to caulk boats. Only in the second half of the nineteenth century were deep wells sunk in the Russian Caucasus and in Pennsylvania in the United States, accompanied by the refining of crude oil into kerosene, used for lighting. By 1910 it was clear that another oil product, gasoline, had beat steam and electricity to become the driving force behind the car, having already enabled the Wright brothers to achieve powered flight. Two years later, Britain's Royal Navy began the long process of converting the fleet from coal- to oil-fired engines.

For Admiral Jacky Fisher, oil's higher power-to-weight ratio offered greater endurance at sea, without calling at coaling stations. Like Germany, Belgium, and France, Britain owed her wealth to an industrial revolution driven by domestic supplies of coal. However, Europe's only oilfields lay in the Carpathian Mountain range. In the absence of domestic supply, oil had to be sought abroad. In 1914, 64% of world production came from the US, with Russia (16%) a distant second, followed by Mexico (7%) and Romania (3%). American exports were controlled by John D. Rockefeller's Standard Oil, a circumstance that many found unsettling.

Other sources were needed. In many cases, the discovery of oil provided delayed justification for expansion which even the most ardent imperialist might otherwise have struggled to explain. Though rubber provided a way to make the Dutch East Indies and Belgian Congo pay (at terrible cost), until commercial oil production began in the Caucasus and Burma (1880s), Persia and Mexico (1900s) and Venezuela (1910s), it was hard to see what exactly the Russian, British, and American empires could find to fight over.

France, Italy, and Germany were laggards. Under Kaiser Wilhelm II, Germany turned towards the Ottoman Empire in the 1890s, seeking to transform a weakness into a strength, presenting itself as a strategic partner without any territorial ambitions in the region. The decade before 1914, the famous Baghdad railway (*Bagdadbahn*) and General Liman van Sanders's military mission saw Germany deploy its financial strength, engineering know-how, and military prowess to knit together an Ottoman Empire whose extremities (Egypt, the Balkans, Libya) had been picked away by other Powers over the previous half century.

What Germany got out of this bargain was unclear. Under a 1904 concession, Deutsche Bank secured oil rights over lands on either side of the railway line, whose course was altered to pass through the most promising areas around Mosul. Once again, oil provided a belated justification for a railway to nowhere.

Fighting

Further down the Tigris, in Persia (Iran), oil was struck much earlier, in 1908, conveniently close to the Persian Gulf. This concession had been granted by the Shah to a Briton, William Knox D'Arcy, in 1901. Like so many before him and since, for years D'Arcy pumped a small fortune into the ground before seeing a profit. Even after the 1908 strike, the Anglo-Persian Oil Company's poor management slowed development. Unable to find a buyer, in 1914 D'Arcy and APOC managing director Charles Greenway pulled off a coup: by threatening to sell out to Shell, Greenway persuaded First Lord of the Admiralty Winston Churchill to give APOC an Admiralty supply contract and purchase a 51% share on behalf of the British government.

The British government's purchase of APOC (today's BP) was hailed as a masterstroke on Churchill's part. In fact, this bail-out proved an embarrassment. If the British 'sailed to victory on a sea of oil', as foreign secretary George Nathaniel Curzon put it, it was not BP's oil. The Admiralty discovered that what little fuel BP's Abadan facility produced turned to jelly in cold temperatures. With Russian oil inaccessible owing to the revolution, it was the much-feared Standard Oil and the much-maligned Shell (whom Greenway said was secretly German-controlled) which kept Allied forces supplied during the war, with American and Mexican oil.

With BP focused on survival, it was left to Shell and Standard to compete for global dominance. While BP nailed its colours to a British mast, these firms changed their colours as circumstances dictated. Thanks to the break-up of Standard Oil in 1911 into a sisterhood of smaller firms and Shell's Anglo-Dutch ownership structure, it was easy for both to hide behind foreign subsidiaries. Remarkably, while Shell had a major subsidiary producing oil within the United States, Shell's lobbying helped delay Standard's entry into Dutch-controlled Indonesia.

A savvy oil company like Shell could make both protectionist and free-trading policies pay. War paid even better: in four years, France's fleet of oil-fuelled trucks,

Portrait of Calouste Gulbenkian by Charles Joseph Watelet, 1912

tractors, tanks, and planes exploded from 316 to 97,279. Admittedly, the war also led governments to set up oil supply agencies such as the French Comité Générale des Pétroles. Rather than being a route to nationalisation, these agencies enabled state capture by the oil firms: they were largely staffed by executives seconded from the oil industry.

Companies making so much money might have behaved nicely to each other. On the contrary, they were not above creating a phoney supply 'crisis', as in 1917, simply to boost market share. By exaggerating the effect of German submarines on transatlantic tankers, Shell claimed, falsely, that France would run out of oil in a matter of months. Shell persuaded the French prime minister Georges Clemenceau to lobby US president Woodrow Wilson to put pressure on Standard Oil to move four of its tankers from the Pacific to the Atlantic. For Shell, it was a matter of defending Asian oil markets against Standard Oil. But for the statesmen and generals, it was something more important.

The latter's perspective was that of the front and the factory, measured in days' supply of gasoline and daily output of TNT. The oil companies' perspective was global market share. The war among these emerging oil 'majors' never stopped, even during the odd negotiated cease-fire. As the oil magnate Calouste Gulbenkian put it, 'oil men are like cats: you never know listening to them whether they are fighting or making love.' Middle Eastern oil played a central role in the shift from cut-throat competition to 'making love'.

Making Love

A polyglot Ottoman-Armenian, Gulbenkian was fond of collecting idioms, including the Dutch *eendracht maakt macht* ('unity is strength'). In the years leading up to the First World War, he observed how rival concession holders prevented each other from developing their claims within the Ottoman Empire: whenever Deutsche Bank's concession seemed to be making progress, American, British, and French ambassadors in Istanbul would pressure the Ottomans to stop. The reverse happened whenever, say, BP's claim seemed to have the grand vizier's favour.

Though Ottomans ranging from local sheikhs to the sultan himself had been staking their own claims for decades, none had the financing or know-how to develop their own oil production. As the brains behind the Turkish Petroleum Company (TPC), established in 1912, Gulbenkian brought rival English and German concession-holders together, ending the stalemate in the 1914 Foreign Office Agreement. Under this remarkable alliance of rivals, Shell, BP, and Deutsche Bank agreed that none of them would seek oil within the confines of 'the Ottoman Empire in Asia' except through TPC, their joint venture.

When one considers that the 'Ottoman Empire in Asia' in 1914 embraced modern-day Iraq, Saudi Arabia, and the Gulf statelets (if not Kuwait or Iran), the Agreement's potential becomes evident. A concession was signed with the Ottomans later that year, giving TPC rights to explore the most promising Ottoman territories around Mosul. Unfortunately, the outbreak of war left both agreements dead in the water. Having entered an alliance with the empire on the very eve of the conflict, the Germans now had the field to themselves, sending their *Brennstoffkommando Arabien* (militarised oil survey) to sink the first modern oil wells in Ottoman Mesopotamia, once again around Mosul. Oil was found, but too late: it was December 1917.

Defeat in Europe ended the Kaiser's dreams of Baghdad, and Deutsche Bank was stripped of its 25% share in TPC under the Treaty of Versailles. Amazingly, this share was offered by the British government to the French, even though France had contributed little to the war effort in the Middle East. Clemenceau's snooty remark that 'when I want some oil, I go to my grocer' suggested a certain indifference

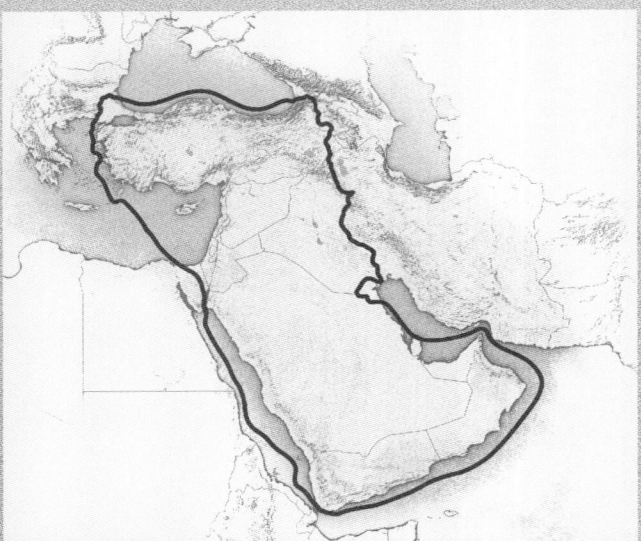

The Red Line Agreement, named after the line delineating the vast area within which the partners of the Turkish Petroleum Company agreed to collaborate, was signed on 31 July 1928 in Ostend (Belgium).

to oil's significance. Under the secret 1916 Anglo-French Sykes-Picot Agreement, oil-rich Mosul (in northern Mesopotamia/Iraq) was allocated to a future French sphere of influence. Yet Clemenceau abandoned France's claim at the request of British premier David Lloyd George in December 1918. The achievement of French officials is therefore remarkable. Having dallied with Shell during the war, in 1920 they decided to allocate the quarter share of TPC to a new company, the Compagnie Française des Pétroles (CFP, established in 1924).

Unable to afford to take its own state share, the French government ensured that shares in CFP were spread among a number of companies, preventing any one from taking control. CFP was little more than a holding company, repeatedly failing to develop sources of oil elsewhere. Yet the surprise post-war allocation of a quarter share in Middle Eastern oil production allowed the French to stay in the oil game. Eventually, after another world war, CFP would finally spread its wings, becoming the oil giant we know as Total. It had been a very close-run thing.

America's Standard Oil was not going to stand by and let Britain and France divide the oily spoils of war between themselves. In 1920 it launched the 'oil war': a public relations campaign which conjured up a British oil 'octopus' intent on world domination, in defiance of what Americans referred to as 'the open door': the freedom to invest one's capital anywhere in the world. The State Department lapped it up, putting diplomatic pressure on London, which in turn pressured BP to let the Americans into both TPC as well as a new venture set up to exploit northern Iran.

Having achieved its aims, the 'oil war' ended: Standard's revenge for the equally artificial 'oil crisis' of 1917. Working out the terms under which Standard would participate in TPC took much longer. Negotiations at Lausanne in 1922–3 delayed matters, raising the possibility that the Americans might find a way to Mosul's oil in collaboration with the new Turkish regime. Many Turks had visions of the blessings that oil-inspired American investment would bring the infant Republic: railways, factories, and high-rise buildings. It was not the last oil-fuelled vision to prove illusory.

Only in 1928 would the Red Line Agreement be reached, named after the line delineating the vast area within which TPC partners agreed to collaborate. TPC had struck oil 100 miles southeast of Mosul the previous October. By adopting a 'go slow' policy on the construction of pipelines necessary to bring the region's oil on stream (Mosul's oil finally reached TPC's Mediterranean terminal at Haifa in 1934), the TPC partners protected their global markets from 'oversupply'. For Iraq and its neighbours, the TPC cartel kept much-needed income from royalties low. Rather than a partnership, many within Iraq saw the relationship as exploitative. 'We wish Iraq to benefit from its resources', noted the Bagdad newspaper İstiklâl in 1923, 'the exploitation of such deposits should leave no ground for foreign interference in the administration of our country.' Distrust of TPC led Ibn Saud to award the concession for his newly established kingdom of Saudi Arabia to an all-American company in 1933; American oil executives ensured that the United States would in time become a firm Saudi ally.

Dream or Nightmare?

The oil of the Middle East did little to power the war effort: only after the second world war did the axis of world oil production shift from the Gulf of Mexico to the Persian Gulf. The rapid

The end of the TPC oil pipeline between Kirkuk (Iraq) and Haifa, Palestine (now Israel), in 1938. At Haifa, crude oil reached the Mediterranean Sea. From there it could be distributed further west. The pipeline, which was 942 kilometres long, was operational between 1935 and 1948.

consolidation of the oil industry during the Great War and its manipulation of host states nonetheless set the terms by which Middle Eastern oil entered world markets. These terms were far removed from the anti-imperialist Fourteen Points advanced by Wilson at the conflict's end. Thanks to Henri Deterding, Walter Teagle, and John Cadman, the leaders of giants we know as Shell, ExxonMobil, and BP the fate of the Middle East lay as much in the hands of oil executives and shareholders as it did in those of presidents and statesmen.

Culturally the Great War saw 'oil' emerge as a symbol with conflicting meanings: for some, 'oil' meant power; for others, exploitation. In 1923 Britain ruled Iraq under a League of Nations mandate, yet many within Britain would have shared *İstiklâl* 's sense of being exploited (as consumers) by the same oil companies' price fixing. Whether conceived as a 'spider', an 'octopus' or something else entirely, by 1923 it was evident that 'oil' was detached from familiar structures of empire and the state. Yet 'oil' also shaped that political order. The resulting conspiracy theories, apocalyptic visions, and moral exhaustion have not left us: indeed, we might say they define the post-truth world we live in today.

Further Reading

'For Civilisation': The First World War in the Middle East, 1914–1923 – Pieter Trogh

Ansary, Tamim (2009). *Destiny Disrupted: A History of the World through Islamic Eyes*. New York: Public Affairs.

Fromkin, David (1989/2004). *A Peace to End All Peace: The Fall of the Ottoman Empire and the Creation of the Modern Middle East*. New York: St. Martin's Press.

Gerwarth, Robert (2016). *The Vanquished: Why the First World War Failed to End, 1917–1923*. London: Allen Lane.

Gingeras, Ryan (2016). *Fall of the Sultanate: The Great War and the End of the Ottoman Empire 1908–1922*. Oxford: Oxford University Press.

Khalidi, Rashid (1998). 'The "Middle East" as a Framework of Analysis: Re-Mapping a Region in the Era of Globalisation', in: *Comparative Studies of South Asia, Africa, and the Middle East* 18 (1), pp. 74–81.

Maalouf, Amin (2010). *De ontregeling van de wereld*. Breda: De Geus, 2010.

Said, Edward (1978). *Orientalism*. New York: Pantheon.

Theodor Wiegand (1864–1936)

McMeekin, Sean (2010). *The Berlin-Baghdad Express. The Ottoman Empire and Germany's Bid for World Power, 1898–1918*. London: Allen Lane.

Belgium and the Ottoman Empire in the Long Nineteenth Century – Houssine Alloul

Alloul, Houssine (2017). 'Belgium and the Ottoman Empire: Diplomacy, Capital, and Transnational Loyalties, 1865–1914', PhD thesis (Universiteit Antwerpen).

Alloul, Houssine, Edhem Eldem, and Henk De Smaele, eds (2018). *To Kill A Sultan: A Transnational History of the Attempt on Abdülhamid II (1905)*. London: Palgrave Macmillan.

Anckaer, Jan (2013). *Small Power Diplomacy and Commerce: Belgium and the Ottoman Empire During the Reign of Leopold I (1831–1865)*. Istanbul: The Isis Press.

Aubert, Roger (1979). 'Les démarches du Cardinal Mercier en vue de l'octroi à la Belgique d'un mandat sur la Palestine', *Classe des Lettres et des Sciences Morales et Politiques et de la Classe des Beaux-Arts. Bulletin*. 5e série, 65 (5), pp. 166–228.

De Beul, Frans (1990). 'La Belgique et la Palestine durant la première guerre mondiale. Une analyse diplomatique', in: Claude Roosens, Albert Bastenier, and Bichara Khader, eds, *La Belgique et le monde arabe*. Louvain-la-Neuve: Academia, pp. 41–62.

De Waele, Maria (1976). 'Een verwaarloosd aspect van de Belgische buitenlandse politiek. De Belgische interesse voor de voogdij over Palestina (1914–1918)', *Belgisch Tijdschrift voor Nieuwste Geschiedenis*, 7 (1–2), pp. 83–111.

Mignon, Laurent (2006). 'Voyageurs ottomans en Belgique et au Luxembourg', in: Laurent Mignon, ed., *Lettres de Turquie et d'ailleurs. Écrits sur des rencontres nécessaires*. Brussels: Memor, pp. 9–32.

Pil, Steven (1997). 'De Belgische diplomatie en de definitieve regeling van de Oosterse Kwestie 1918–1922', MA thesis (Universiteit Gent).

Thobie, Jacques (1974). 'Intérêts belges et intérêts français dans l'Empire Ottoman (1880–1914)', in: *Les relations franco-belges de 1830 à 1934. Actes du Colloque de Metz*. Metz: Université de Metz, pp. 213–44.

Van den Reeck, Marc (2000). *Belgium in the Ottoman Capital, From the Early Steps to 'La Belle Époque': The Centenary of 'Le Palais de Belgique', 1900–2000*. Istanbul: Consulaat Generaal van België.

Verbruggen, Thomas (2015). 'Under The Moon and the Stars: The Impact of the Great War on the Ottoman Sephardic Community in Antwerp (1870–1930)', MA thesis (Universiteit Antwerpen).

Yetişgin, Memet, and Toroshan Özdamar (2018). 'Osmanlı şehirlerinde Belçika şirketlerinin altyapı faaliyetleri', *Tarih Araştırmaları Dergisi*, 36 (64), pp. 373–408.

From Declarations of War to Armistice— The First World War in the Middle East, 1914–1918 – Pieter Trogh

Aksakal, Mustafa (2010). *The Ottoman Road to War in 1914. The Ottoman Empire and the First World War*. Cambridge: Cambridge University Press.

Deringil, Selim (2019). *The Ottoman Twilight in the Arab lands. Turkish Memoirs and Testimonies of the Great War*. Boston: Academic Studies Press.

Faulkner, Neil (2016). *Lawrence of Arabia's War. The Arabs, the British and the Remaking of the Middle East in WWI*. New Haven: Yale University Press.

Fawaz, Leila (2014). *The Land of Aching Hearts. The Middle East in the Great War*. Cambridge, MA: Harvard University Press.

Fromkin, David (1989/2009). *A Peace to End All Peace. The Fall of the Ottoman Empire and the Creation of the Modern Middle East*. New York: St. Martin's Press.

Gingeras, Ryan (2016). *Fall of the Sultanate. The Great War and the End of the Ottoman Empire 1908–1922*. Oxford: Oxford University Press.

McMeekin, Sean (2010). *The Berlin-Baghdad Express. The Ottoman Empire and Germany's Bid for World Power, 1898–1918*. London: Allen Lane.

Travers, Tim (2004). *Gallipoli, 1915*. Stroud: Tempus.

Üngör, Uğur Ümit (2012). *The Making of Modern Turkey. Nation and State in Eastern Anatolia, 1913–1950*. Oxford: Oxford University Press.

Zürcher, Eric-Jan, ed. (2015). *Jihad and Islam in World War I: Studies on the Ottoman Jihad at the Centenary of Snouck Hurgronje's 'Holy War Made in Germany'*. Leiden: Leiden University Press.

Falih Rıfkı (1894–1971)

Atay, Falih Rıfkı (1932). *Zeytindağı* [Mount of Olives, Memories of World War I in Syria and Palestine].

Deringil, Selim (2019). *The Ottoman Twilight in the Arab Lands. Turkish Memoirs and Testimonies of the Great War*. Boston: Academic Studies Press.

Wavell's Eye. Connections between Flanders Fields and the Middle East in the First World War – Pieter Trogh

Chielens, Piet, and Dominiek Dendooven (2008). *World War I. Five Continents in Flanders*. Tielt: Lannoo.

Chielens, Piet, and Pieter Trogh (2016). *De Geschreven Oorlog. Anthologie van teksten van het front in België 1914–1940*. Antwerp: Manteau.

Fantauzzo, Justin (2020). *The Other Wars. The Experience and Memory of the First World War in the Middle East and Macedonia*. Cambridge: Cambridge University Press.

Trogh, Pieter (2019). *De Namenlijst, een algemene inleiding. Naar een inclusieve geschiedenis en herdenking van de Eerste Wereldoorlog in België*. Ypres: In Flanders Fields Museum.

Woodward, David R. (2006). *Forgotten Soldiers of the First World War*. Cheltenham: The History Press Ltd.

Frank Hurley (1885–1962)

Dixon, Robert, and Christopher Lee (2011). *The Diaries of Frank Hurley: 1912–1941*. Melbourne: Anthem Press.

Hurley, Daniel, and Frank O'Keefe (1986). *Hurley at War. The Photography and Diaries of Frank Hurley in Two World Wars*. Fairfax: Fairfax Library.

Shenorhig Tenguerian (1905–?)

https://www.houshamadyan.org/oda/europe/der-meguerditchian-coll-ger.html

https://www.silvina-der-meguerditchian.de/works/the-texture-of-identity-ongoing/

Gendered Violence against Children during the Armenian Genocide – Nazan Maksudyan

Bjørnlund, M. (2009). '"A Fate Worse Than Dying": Sexual Violence during the Armenian Genocide', in: D. Herzog, ed., *Brutality and Desire: War and Sexuality in Europe's Twentieth Century*. Basingstoke: Springer.

Ekmekçioğlu, L. (2013). 'A Climate for Abduction, a Climate for Redemption: The Politics of Inclusion during and after the Armenian Genocide', *Comparative Studies in Society and History* 55/3, pp. 522–3.

Elliott, M. E. (1924). *Beginning Again at Ararat*. New York: Fleming H. Revell Company.

Haigaz, A. (2015). *Four Years in the Mountains of Kurdistan: An Armenian Boy's Memoir of Survival*. Translated by I. Haigaz Chekenian. Bronxville, New York: Maiden Lane Press.

Kieser, H.-L. (2018). *Talaat Pasha: The Father of Modern Turkey, Architect of Genocide*. Princeton: Princeton University Press.

Maksudyan, N. (2019). *Ottoman Children and Youth during World War I*. Syracuse, NY: Syracuse University Press.

Miller, D. E. and Touryan Miller, L. (1993). *Survivors: An Oral History of the Armenian Genocide*. Berkeley: University of California Press.

Panian, K. (2015 [1992]). *Goodbye, Antoura: A Memoir of the Armenian Genocide*. Translated in an abridged form from the Armenian by S. Beugekian. Stanford: Stanford University Press.

Sarafian, A. (2001). 'The Absorption of Armenian Women and Children into Muslim Households as a Structural Component of the Armenian Genocide', in: Omer Bartov and Phyllis Mack, eds, *In God's Name: Genocide and Religion in the Twentieth Century*. New York: Berghahn Books, pp. 209–21.

Suny, R. G. (2015). 'Armenian Genocide', in: Ute Daniel et al., eds, *1914-1918-online. International Encyclopedia of the First World War*. Freie Universität Berlin: Berlin, 2015-05-26. DOI: 10.15463/ie1418.10646.

Watenpaugh, K. D. (2013). '"Are There Any Children for Sale?": Genocide and the Transfer of Armenian Children (1915–1922)', *Journal of Human Rights* 12/3, pp. 283–95.

Ze'evi, D., and B. Morris (2019). *The Thirty-Year Genocide: Turkey's Destruction of its Christian Minorities, 1894–1924*. Cambridge: Harvard University Press.

Ihsan Turjman (1893–1917)

Tamari, Salim (2015). *Year of the Locust. A Soldier's Diary and the Erasure of Palestine's Ottoman Past*. Berkeley, CA: University of California Press.

Between Imperialism and Revolution: Geopolitics of the Great War in the Middle East – Alp Yenen

Aksakal, Mustafa (2008). *The Ottoman Road to War in 1914: The Ottoman Empire and the First World War*. Cambridge: Cambridge University Press.

Gingeras, Ryan (2016). *Fall of the Sultanate: The Great War and the End of the Ottoman Empire, 1908–1922*. Oxford: Oxford University Press.

Fromkin, David (1989). *A Peace to End All Peace: The Fall of the Ottoman Empire and the Creation of the Modern Middle East*. 20th year anniversary edition. New York: Henry Holt & Co., 2009.

Motadel, David, ed. (2014). *Islam and the European Empires*. Oxford: Oxford University Press.

Öztan, Ramazan Hakkı (2018). 'Point of No Return? Prospects of Empire After the Ottoman Defeat in the Balkan Wars (1912–1913)', *International Journal of Middle East Studies* 50 (1), pp. 65–84.

Reynolds, Michael A. (2011). *Shattering Empires: The Clash and Collapse of the Ottoman and Russian Empires 1908–1918*. Cambridge: Cambridge University Press.

Üngör, Uğur Ümit (2011). *The Making of Modern Turkey: Nation and State in Eastern Anatolia, 1913–50*. Oxford: Oxford University Press.

Yenen, Alp (2021). 'Envisioning Turco-Arab Co-Existence Between Empire and Nationalism', *Die Welt des Islams* 61 (1), pp. 72–112. https://doi.org/10.1163/15700607-00600A17

Yenen, Alp, and Ramazan Hakkı Öztan (2021). 'Age of Rogues: Transgressive Politics at the Frontiers of the Ottoman Empire', in: Ramazan Öztan and Alp Yenen, eds, *Age of Rogues: Rebels, Revolutionaries, and Racketeers at the Frontiers of Empires*, pp. 3–52. Edinburgh: Edinburgh University Press. https://hdl.handle.net/1887/3210518

Zürcher, Erik Jan, ed. (2015). *Jihad and Islam in World War I: Studies on the Ottoman Jihad at the Centenary of Snouck Hurgronje's 'Holy War Made in Germany'*. Leiden: Leiden University Press. https://doi.org/10.26530/OAPEN_605452

Faisal (1882–1933)

Thompson, Elizabeth F. (2020). *How the West Stole Democracy from the Arabs: The Syrian Congress of 1920 and the Destruction of its Historic Liberal-Islamic Alliance*. New York: Grove Press.

The Pillars of Belief: T. E. Lawrence and the Archaeology of the Arab Revolt, 1916–2014 – Nicholas J. Saunders

Barr, J. (2006). *Setting the Desert on Fire: T. E. Lawrence and Britain's Secret War in Arabia, 1916–1918*. London: Bloomsbury.

Berton, J. (2011). *T. E. Lawrence and the Arab Revolt: An Illustrated Guide*. Madrid: Andrea Press.

Faulkner, N. (2016). *Lawrence of Arabia's War*. London: Yale University Press.

Lawrence, T. E. (2003). *Seven Pillars of Wisdom, a Triumph. The Complete 1922 Text*. (Second edition with amendments. Jeremy and Nicole Wilson). Fordingbridge: Castle Hill Press.

Mousa, S. (1966). *T.E. Lawrence: An Arab View*. London: Oxford University Press.

Nicholson, J. (2005). *The Hejaz Railway*. London: Stacey International.

Özyüksel, M. (2014). *The Hejaz Railway and the Ottoman Empire: Modernity, Industrialisation, and the Ottoman Decline*. London: I. B. Tauris.

Rogan, E. (2015). *The Fall of the Ottomans: The Great War in the Middle East, 1914–1920*. London: Allen Lane.

Saunders, N. J. (2020). *Desert Insurgency: Archaeology, T. E. Lawrence, & the Arab Revolt*. Oxford: Oxford University Press.

Walker, P. (2018). *Behind the Lawrence Legend: The Forgotten Few Who Shaped the Arab Revolt*. Oxford: Oxford University Press.

Wilson, J. (1990). *Lawrence of Arabia: The Authorised Biography*. London: Minerva.

Sèvres, Lausanne, and the Invention of the Middle East – Ozan Ozavci

Fraser, T. G., ed. (2015). *The First World War and its Aftermath: The Shaping of the Modern Middle East*. London: Gingko Library.

Provence, Michael (2017). *The Last Ottoman Generation and the Making of the Modern Middle East*. Cambridge: Cambridge University Press.

Smith, Leonard (2018). *Sovereignty at the Paris Peace Conference of 1919*. Oxford: Oxford University Press.

Thompson, Elizabeth (2020). *How the West Stole Democracy from the Arabs: The Syrian Congress of 1920 and the Destruction of its Liberal-Islamic Alliance*. London: Grove Press.

Winter, Jay (2023). *The Day the Great War Ended, 24 July 1923: The Civilianization of War*. Oxford: Oxford University Press.

Halide Edib (1884–1964)

Adivar, Halide Edib (1923). *Memoirs of Halide Edib*. London: John Murray.

Thompson, Elizabeth F. (2013). 'Halide Edib, Turkey's Joan of Arc. The Fate of Liberalism after World War I', in: Elizabeth F. Thompson, *Justice Interrupted. The Struggle for Constitutional Government in the Middle East*. Cambridge, MA: Harvard University Press, pp. 91–116.

The Arab Liberal Revolutions of 1919 and the Violent Consequences of European Suppression – Elizabeth F. Thompson

Aksakal, Mustafa (2014). 'The Ottoman Empire', in: Jay Winter, ed., *The Cambridge History of the First World War: Volume I Global War*. Cambridge: Cambridge University Press, pp. 459–78.

Baron, Beth (2005). *Egypt as a Woman: Nationalism, Gender, and Politics*. Berkeley: University of California Press.

Berque, Jacques (1972). *Egypt: Imperialism and Revolution*. Translated by Jean Stewart. New York: Praeger, 1972.

Fahmy, Ziad (2011). *Ordinary Egyptians: Creating the Modern Nation through Popular Culture*. Stanford: Stanford University Press.

Hassett, Dónal (2019). *Mobilizing Memory: The Great War and the Language of Politics in Algeria, 1918–1939*. Oxford: Oxford University Press.

Kadhim, Abbas (2012). *Reclaiming Iraq: The 1920 Revolution and the Founding of the Modern State*. Austin: University of Texas Press.

Manela, Erez (2007). *The Wilsonian Moment: Self-Determination and the International Origins of Anticolonial Nationalism*. New York: Oxford University Press.

Rida, Muhammad Rashid (1922). 'The European Trip, Part 5,' *al-Manar* 23 (July 1922) pp. 553–60.

Thompson, Elizabeth F. (2021). *How the West Stole Democracy from the Arabs: The Syrian Congress of 1920 and the Destruction of its Historic Liberal-Islamic Alliance*. New York: Grove Press.

Wyrtzen, Jonathan (2022) [forthcoming]. *Worldmaking After World War I*. New York: Columbia University Press.

Victor and Vanquished: Contested War Memory in the Middle East – Bruce Scates

Barrett, Michele (2011). 'Afterword Death and the Afterlife: Britain's Colonies and Dominions', in: Santu Das, ed., *Race, Empire and First World War Writing*. Cambridge: Cambridge University Press, pp. 301–20.

Commonwealth War Graves Commission (2021). *Report of the Special Committee to Review Historical Inequalities in Commemoration*. Maidenhead: Commonwealth War Graves Commission.

Fuchs, Ron (2004). 'Sites of Memory in the Holy Land: The design of the British War Cemeteries in Mandate Palestine', *Journal of Historical Geography* 30, pp. 643–4.

Kieser, Hans-Lukas, Pearl Nunn, and Thomas Schmutz (2022). *Remembering the Great War in the Middle East: From Turkey and Armenia to Australia and New Zealand*. London: I. B. Tauris.

Longworth, Philip (2010). *The Unending Vigil—The History of the Commonwealth War Graves Commission*. Barnsley: Pen and Sword.

Scates, Bruce (2006). *Return to Gallipoli: Walking the Cemeteries of the Great War*. Cambridge: Cambridge University Press.

Unwalla, Pheroze (2018). 'Bereavement and Mourning (Ottoman Empire/Middle East)'. https://encyclopedia.1914-1918-online.net/article/bereavement_and_mourning_ottoman_empire_middle_east

George Knox (1881–1916)

Saunders, Nicholas J. (2004). *Matters of Conflict. Material Culture, Memory and the First World War*. London: Routledge. https://dulwichcollege1914-18.co.uk/fallen/knox-g/

The First World War and the Zionist-Palestinian Conflict, 1914–1948 – Dotan Halevy

Çiçek, M. Talha (2014). *War and State Formation in Syria: Cemal Pasha's Governorate During World War I, 1914–1917*. London, New York: Routledge.

De-Ballobar, Conde [Manzano, Eduardo Moreno, and Roberto Mazza, eds] (2011). *Jerusalem in World War I: The Palestine Diary of a European Diplomat*. New York: I. B. Tauris.

Dolev, Eran, Yigal Sheffy, and Haim Goren, eds (2014). *Palestine and World War I: Grand Strategy, Military Tactics, and Culture in War*. London: I. B. Tauris.

Jacobson, Abigail (2011). *From Empire to Empire: Jerusalem Between Ottoman and British Rule*. Syracuse, NY: Syracuse University Press.

Khalidi, Rashid (1998). *Palestinian Identity: The Construction of Modern National Consciousness*. New York: Columbia University Press.

Mazza, Roberto (2013). *Jerusalem: From the Ottomans to the British*. Reprint edition. London, New York: I. B. Tauris.

Rogan, Eugene (2015). *The Fall of the Ottomans: The Great War in the Middle East*. New York: Basic Books.

Tamari, Salim, and Ihsan Salih Turjman (2015). *Year of the Locust: A Soldier's Diary and the Erasure of Palestine's Ottoman Past*. Oakland, CA: University of California Press.

Tamari, Salim (2017). *The Great War and the Remaking of Palestine*. Oakland, CA: University of California Press.

Wasif Jawhariyyeh (1897–1972)

Tamari, Salim, and Nassar Issam (2014). *The Storyteller of Jerusalem. The Life and Times of Wasif Jawhariyyeh, 1904–1948*. Northampton, MA: Olive Branch Press.

The Kurds and World War I – Djene R. Bajalan

Ahmad, Kamal Mazhar (1994). *Kurdistan during the First World War*. London: Saqi Books.

Akçam, Taner (2017). *The Young Turks' Crime against Humanity: The Armenian Genocide and Ethnic Cleansing in the Ottoman Empire*. Princeton: Princeton University Press.

Bozarslan, Hamit, Cengiz Guneş, and Veli Yadirgi (2021). *The Cambridge History of the Kurds*. Cambridge: Cambridge University Press.

McDowall, David (2021). *A Modern History of the Kurds*. London, I. B. Tauris.

Özoğlu, Hakan (2004). *Kurdish Notables and the Ottoman State: Evolving Identities, Competing Loyalties, and Shifting Boundaries*. Albany: State University of New York Press.

Reynolds, Michael (2014). *Shattering Empires: The Clash and Collapse of the Ottoman and Russian Empires, 1908–1918*. Cambridge: Cambridge University Press.

Soleimani, Kamal (2016). *Islam and Competing Nationalisms in the Middle East, 1876–1926*. New York: Palgrave Macmillan.

Strohmeier, Martin (2005). *Crucial Images in the Presentation of a Kurdish National Identity: Heroes and Patriots, Traitors and Foes*. Leiden: Brill.

Üngör, Ugur Ümit (2012). *The Making of Modern Turkey: Nation and State in Eastern Anatolia, 1913–1950*. Oxford: Oxford University Press.

Gertrude Bell (1868–1926)

Gertrude Bell Archive: http://www.gerty.ncl.ac.uk/

Oil: A Crude History of the Great War – Jonathan Conlin

Bouguen, J-M. (2013). *Le pétrole en France: Genèse et stratégies d'influence (1917–1924)*. Paris: L'Harmattan.

Conlin, J. (2019). *Mr Five Per Cent: The Many Lives of Calouste Gulbenkian, the World's Richest Man*. London: Profile.

Fursenko, H. H. (1990). *The Battle for Oil: The Economics and Politics of International Corporate Conflict over Petroleum, 1860–1930*. Translated by Gregory L. Freeze. Greenwich: Jai Press.

Mitchell, T. (2011). *Carbon Democracy: Political Power in the Age of Oil*. London: Verso.

Nowell, G. (1994). *Mercantile States and the World Oil Cartel, 1900–1939*. Ithaca, NY: Cornell University Press.

Stivers, W. (1982). *Supremacy and Oil: Iraq, Turkey, and the Anglo-American World Order, 1918–1930*. Ithaca, NY: Cornell University Press.

Venn, F. (1986). *Oil Diplomacy in the Twentieth Century*. Basingstoke: Macmillan.

About the authors

Houssine Alloul is Assistant Professor of Modern Global History at the University of Amsterdam. He specializes in international history with a focus on Modern Europe and the Late Ottoman Empire. He is co-editor of *To Kill a Sultan: A Transnational History of the Attempt on Abdülhamid II (1905)* (Palgrave, 2018) and, at present, working on a book manuscript on Belgian-Ottoman encounters throughout the long nineteenth century.

Djene R. Bajalan is Associate Professor at Missouri State University. He specializes on the history of the Middle East, with a focus on the rise of nationalism and the evolution of the Kurdish question. He is the author of numerous works on Kurdish history, including *Jön Kürtler: Birinci Dünya Savaşı'ndan Önce Kürt Hareketi, 1898-1914* (2010). He is also an editor at the journal *Kurdish Studies*.

Jonathan Conlin teaches history at the University of Southampton, and is co-founder of The Lausanne Project, a forum for the latest research in, and comment on, the legacies of the 1923 Treaty of Lausanne. In 2019 he published *Mr Five Per Cent*, a biography of the Anglo-Armenian oil magnate, financier and art collector Calouste Gulbenkian (1869-1955), that won the BAC Wadsworth Prize for Business History.

Dotan Halevy is a Polonsky postdoctoral fellow in the Van Leer Institute, Jerusalem. His research focuses on the culture, society, and environment of the modern Middle East. His doctoral dissertation, entitled "Stripped: Ruination, Liminality, and the Making of the Gaza Strip 1840-1950", was completed at Columbia University, and offers a modern history of the Gaza borderland under Ottoman and British rule.

Nazan Maksudyan is a Senior Researcher at the Centre Marc Bloch (Berlin) and visiting professor at the Friedrich-Meinecke-Institut at the Freie Universität Berlin. Her research mainly focuses on the social and cultural history of the late Ottoman Empire (from the 18th to 20th centuries) and modern Turkey, with special interest in children and youth, gender, sexuality, and the history of sciences.

Pieter Trogh is an historian and scientific collaborator at the In Flanders Fields Museum in Ypres (Belgium). He has published on different aspects of the First World War. With Piet Chielens he co-authored *'De Geschreven Oorlog': een anthologie van teksten van het front in België 1914-1940* (Antwerp: Manteau, 2016). In 2022 he was the curator of the temporary exhibition *'For Civilisation'. The First World War in the Middle East, 1914-1923.*

Ozan Ozavci is an Assistant professor in the History of International Relations at the University of Utrecht. Dr. Ozavci works on Euro-Middle Eastern relations from the late eighteenth century until the 1950s. His latest book, *Dangerous Gifts: Imperialism, Security, and Civil Wars in the Levant, 1798-1864* was published by Oxford University Press in 2021.

Nicholas J. Saunders is an academic archaeologist and anthropologist and Emeritus Professor of Material Culture in the Department of Anthropology and Archaeology at the University of Bristol. He is a prominent contributor to the field of modern conflict archaeology, and has authored and edited numerous academic publications, including *Desert Insurgency: Archaeology, T.E. Lawrence, and the Arab Revolt*, published by Oxford University Press in 2020.

Bruce Scates is a historian, academic, novelist and documentary film producer at the Australian National University. He is the lead author of *Anzac Journeys* (Cambridge University Press) and a contributor to the *Cambridge History of the First World War*. His work covers a wide range of historical fields including war commemoration, the memory of conflict, and the politics of memorialization.

Elizabeth F. Thompson is Mohamed S. Farsi Chair of Islamic Peace and Professor of History at the American University, Washington, D.C. Her research focuses on the history of social movements and liberal constitutionalism in the Middle East. In 2021 she published *How the West Stole Democracy from the Arabs: The Syrian Congress of 1920 and the Destruction of its Historic Liberal-Islamic Alliance* (New York: Grove Press).

Alp Yenen is an Assistant Professor for modern Turkish history and culture at the Leiden University Institute for Area Studies. He works primarily on the political history of the modern Middle East in international and transnational relations. His last book is an edited volume titled *Age of Rogues: Rebels, Revolutionaries and Racketeers at the Frontiers of Empires*, published by Edinburgh University Press in 2021.

Photographic credits

The publisher has made every effort to comply with copyright rules but has not been able to identify the copyright holders for every image reproduced in this book. Anyone who believes his or her rights have been overlooked is requested to contact the publisher.

All images were made available to the publisher by In Flanders Fields Museum.

Numbers refer to pages, letters to the place on the page (clockwise).

Algemeen Rijksarchief, Brussels: p. 27b
Archives de la Service historique de la Défense, Vincennes : p. 134
Collection Joseph Berton, Chicago: p. 34, 35b, 48, 49, 50ab, 72b, 73, 119
Collection Mitchell Library, State Library of New South Wales: p. 8a, 45ab, 46abcd, 47ab, 64–65, 66a, 67, 70, 71
Collection Palestine Exploration Fund, London: pp. 66b, 100–101, 121, 138–139, 148
Collection Silvina Der-Meguerditchian, Berlin: p. 76
Collection Turjman Family: p. 84
Collection Vahe Tachjian: pp. 78, 82, 83, 108
Courtesy Archives New Zealand/Te Rua Mahara o te Kawantanga: p. 162a
Courtesy Australian War Memorial: p. 163
Courtesy Calouste Gulbenkian Foundation: p. 185
Courtesy of Sabine Réth & Art Libre: p. 8b
Courtesy Nicholas J. Saunders: p. 98ab

Courtesy Bruce Scates: p. 161
Department of Defense, Melbourne, Australia: p. 160
Dulwich College, London: p. 164
In Flanders Fields Museum, Ypres: pp. 10, 14, 16, 17, 18, 19, 20a, 21
In Flanders Fields Museum, Ypres, Collection Antony (© 2022 Antony / IFFM, Ieper): p. 165
Library of Congress, Washington: front cover, pp. 2–3, 9, 11, 13, 15, 20b, 23, 32, 37ab, 51, 52, 53, 54, 55, 56abc, 57, 58ab, 59, 61, 62, 72a, 77, 85a, 89a, 96a, 97, 99, 102, 103, 104, 105, 109, 110, 111, 112, 113, 114–115, 117, 129ab, 132b, 136, 140–141, 142ab, 143, 144, 145, 149ab, 150, 152–153, 154, 155, 156–157, 158, 166, 168, 169, 170, 171, 173, 181, 182
Private collection: pp. 26b, 28ab, 29a, 40b, 118, 136, 146, 151
Wiki Commons: pp. 12, 22, 33ab, 35a, 36, 38, 40a, 41, 42, 43, 44, 60, 63, 68–69, 74–75, 80, 81, 85b, 86, 88ab, 90, 92, 93, 96b, 106, 107, 116, 124, 125, 126, 127, 128, 132a, 133a, 135, 147, 162b, 172, 176, 177, 179, 180, 187
www.egypt2011andbeyond.blogspot.com: p. 133b

This book was published on the occasion of the exhibition

'For Civilisation'.
The First World War in the Middle East, 1914–1923

In Flanders Fields Museum, Ypres
12 March–2 October 2022

Publishers
Tijdsbeeld, Ghent
Director: Ronny Gobyn

In Flanders Fields Museum, Ypres
Director: Stephen Lodewyck

Copy-editing
Irene Schaudies

Translation
Lee Preedy (texts by Pieter Trogh and Houssine Alloul)

Design
Janpieter Chielens

Picture research and maps
Pieter Trogh
Janpieter Chielens

Editorial management
Ann Mestdag, Tijdsbeeld, Gent

Colour correction, printing and binding
Graphius, Gent

Typeset in Artifex CF en Nimbus Sans
Printed on op MagnoVolume 150g

© 2022 TIJDSBEELD, Ghent / In Flanders Fields Museum, Ypres / and the authors

ISBN 978-94-9088-034-7
D/2022/9045/3

In Flanders Fields Museum
https://www.inflandersfields.be

TIJDSBEELD Publishing
www.tijdsbeeld.be

Distribution
Exhibitions International
www.exhibitionsinternational.be

All rights reserved. No part of this publication may be reproduced or transmitted, in any form or by any means, without the prior permission in writing from the publisher.

The exhibition and publication were made possible thanks to the support of

Front cover:
An orphaned Armenian boy, survivor of the genocide, c. 1921

Pages 2-3:
El-Salt (present-day As-Salt, Jordan) 20 August 1921. The local population listens to the declaration of the British High Commissioner Herbert Samuel following the foundation of Transjordan.